"Jenné Claiborne has done it again—easy, delicious, and very good vegan recipes!"

—TABITHA BROWN,
New York Times bestselling author
of *Cooking from the Spirit*

"Jenné Claiborne has created a cookbook that is both inspiring and practical, a balance I've needed as a new mom. The whole family (kids included!) will love easy weeknight dishes like Black Bean Crust Pizza—and you can whip up her Better Buttermilk Waffles on the weekend. Yes, please!"

—JESSICA HYLTON,
creator of Jessica in the Kitchen

"Jenné Claiborne's creativity shines in *Sweet Potato Soul Vegan Vibes*! She brings a fresh and exciting approach to vegan cooking. Each recipe is a celebration of plant-based ingredients."

—NISHA VORA, creator of Rainbow
Plant Life and author of *Big Vegan Flavor*

"Jenné Claiborne's *Sweet Potato Soul Vegan Vibes* is a celebration of all things plant-based. Her recipes are innovative, flavorful, and sure to please everyone at the table. You won't miss a thing—instead, you'll be coming back for seconds!"

—NISHA MELVANI, creator of
Cooking for Peanuts and
author of *Practically Vegan*

"Eating vegan doesn't have to be boring, and *Sweet Potato Soul Vegan Vibes* by Jenné Claiborne proves it. In her second cookbook, Claiborne transforms divine soul food favorites into nourishing, delicious, and approachable plant-based dishes you'll want to make on repeat. With stunning food photography and recipes written by a plant-based legend, this is a must-have cookbook for vegans and non-vegans alike!"

—CARLEIGH BODRUG, *New York Times* bestselling author of *PlantYou*

sweet potato soul

vegan vibes

sweet potato soul

vegan vibes

100 SOULFUL PLANT-BASED RECIPES
FOR HEALTHY EVERYDAY MEALS

jenné claiborne

RODALE

NEW YORK

By Jenné Claiborne
Sweet Potato Soul
Sweet Potato Soul Vegan Vibes

Published in the United States by Rodale Books, an imprint of Random House,
a division of Penguin Random House LLC, New York.

RODALE and the Plant colophon are registered trademarks of
Penguin Random House LLC.

Library of Congress Cataloging-in-Publication Data
Names: Claiborne, Jenné, author.
Title: Sweet potato soul vegan vibes / Jenné Claiborne.
Description: First edition. | New York, NY : Rodale, [2025] | Includes index.
Identifiers: LCCN 2024012654 (print) | LCCN 2024012655 (ebook) |
ISBN 9780593581551 (hardcover) | ISBN 9780593581568 (ebook)
Subjects: LCSH: Vegan cooking. | Cooking (Natural foods) | LCGFT: Cookbooks.
Classification: LCC TX837 .C4979 2025 (print) | LCC TX837 (ebook) |
DDC 641.5/6362--dc23/eng/20240410
LC record available at https://lccn.loc.gov/2024012654
LC ebook record available at https://lccn.loc.gov/2024012655

Printed in China

RodaleBooks.com | RandomHouseBooks.com

2 4 6 8 9 7 5 3 1

First Edition

Book design by Allison Chi

For Jorji

Contents

Brilliant Breakfasts

Fun & Fancy Apps & Snacks

Super-Satisfying Salads & Soups

Everyday Entrées

Divine Desserts

Better Beverages

Save These Sauces & Flavor-Makers

Introduction

You'll know a vegan vibe when you feel it: an energy that's bright, positive, balanced, clear, and thriving.

I've had these feelings since becoming vegan in 2011. Sure, there are days when I feel exhausted and dull from the grind of work and parenting, but it's been my experience that my happy medium always comes back to harmony and joy. When I'm eating the best plant-based foods, staying hydrated, and moving my body, the dull moments don't last long.

A SUCCESSFUL VEGAN IS HEALTHY, VIBRANT, AND COLORFUL. At least that has been my experience, and the experience of many vegans around the world. Vegan living and eating should be fun, exciting, and always delicious. The food should nourish and fuel your body, but also your soul. You deserve to thrive and operate at your personal best every day.

When I went vegan, the stereotype was that plant-based food was boring and bland. But those days are over. Vegan food has never been more delicious, diverse, and accessible, with restaurants and grocery aisles devoted to plant-based cuisine. At the same time, though, vegan food has never been more processed. Ultraprocessed foods like faux meats and cheeses make it easier for millions of people to eat less meat, but our reliance on these foods can make it harder to really dive into the wonderful world of nutritious and delicious plants.

A good vegan diet does not mimic the Standard American Diet. This cookbook aims to teach you how to make incredible, tasty food with nature's most nutritious ingredients: plants. And it is my goal to make the best of vegan eating attainable no matter how busy you are, where you live, or whether or not you are an avid home cook. The recipes are approachable, fun, and delicious; always delicious. And the best part is, vegan vibes are for you whether you're a full-time vegan or not. Do I want you to be vegan? Of course I do. But I'll let the recipes and this cookbook be your inspiration. My goal is to help you find joy in the kitchen, eat more plants, and catch a vegan vibe!

My Vegan Story

My vegan journey began in 2007 when I was a junior at Boston University. At this time in my life, the only vegans I had met were the Hebrew Israelites in my family whose religion mandated a strict plant-based diet. My idea of health food was Splenda, Coke Zero, and 100-calorie packs of Oreo Thins. A journey must begin somewhere!

I was living off campus for the first time, and sharing a house with three random men in their twenties. You won't be shocked to hear that my male roommates hardly ever set foot in the kitchen—which was fully stocked with everything a new home cook could ask for. So it became my domain. At this time in history, food blogs were starting to give magazines a run for their money, and I fell right into their embrace. I was studying acting in college and had big plans to become the next Halle Berry. With less than two years until graduation, I realized I needed to start eating healthy if I wanted to become the movie star I was born to be. Nice kitchen, food bloggers disrupting food media, and movie star dreams: the perfect storm that changed my life forever.

Let me also state that as a kid, I had been the pickiest eater in the state of Georgia. I required my food to be cooked to just the right doneness, texture, and temperature. I only liked a few fruits, and even fewer vegetables. Nuts, never! Crust on my sandwich, an abomination! Food touching on the plate, forget about it. I didn't taste the majority of the simple everyday plants I use in this cookbook until I was in my twenties. That's why 2007 was such a momentous year for my life and career, which has been totally consumed by food since then.

The first step I took in my healthy eating journey was to give up sugar. Giving up sugar remains trendy to this day, but I don't subscribe to that lifestyle now ... and I gave up sugar in the worst possible way. Splenda was having a moment, so I replaced all the sugar in my diet with artificial sweeteners. For months I ate oatmeal sweetened with SPLENDA! (Don't worry, I now realize the error in my ways!)

As my taste buds developed, so did my ability to detect bullshit. Before long I had discovered the Copley Square Farmers Market in Boston. It was the first farmers' market I ever visited, and the place where my interest in food was truly born. I was confronted with beautiful produce I had never seen before: butternut squash, celery root, golden beets, and kale. One visit and I was hooked. I went straight to Google to learn how to cook this gorgeous produce, and started watching Food Network religiously when I got home from class and rehearsals. If you know me, you'll know I always have a hobby, but this hobby was the first and only to really stick!

Within a few months I was making almost all my own food from scratch, eating vegetables I wouldn't have touched a year prior, and shopping at the farmers' market weekly. I had even kicked Splenda and was sweetening my oatmeal with real maple syrup. I wasn't a vegan, and had zero aspirations to become one, but I see that time as the start of something that eventually changed my life.

Fast-forward to 2011, I was working at a vegan restaurant, Peacefood, on New York City's Upper West Side, living my best *mostly* vegan life, and creating recipes for my own food blog, Sweet Potato Soul. After a year of working there I started to feel guilty every time I ate an animal product. Even a slice of New York pizza would make me feel like I was doing something terribly wrong.

See, up until that point I had flip-flopped between being a vegetarian and a pescatarian. I loved fish and didn't understand why I should stop eating it. I was surrounded by ethical and health vegans but I wasn't ready to hear their message. A few months into feeling guilty about eating animal products, I decided to educate myself on the animal agriculture industry (meat, dairy, fishing, and eggs). I read *Veganist* by Kathy Freston and never looked back. I was now a certified vegan. We'll go into more reasons why you may want to go vegan in future chapters; the reasons are many. I became vegan for the animals (an ethical vegan), but I quickly recognized the benefits to my health and the environment as well.

Did I catch a vegan vibe? You know I did! Within months of becoming vegan, the digestive issues I had suffered from my whole life disappeared (dairy allergy), my acne cleared up, my mood improved, and I had a newfound purpose in my life. Not six weeks into being vegan I had an epiphany: My purpose in life is to help other people discover the joy, vibrancy, and health that comes from eating and living this way. Spread vegan vibes around the world!

A decade-plus into my life as a vegan, some things have changed. I became a professional vegan chef, health coach, and cooking instructor. I've built a successful online food brand, I'm now a single mom living in my hometown of Atlanta, and my life is at least 700 percent more complicated than it was when I started this journey. The one constant through it all has been my vegan diet and lifestyle. That's something that I love about this lifestyle; it will meet you where you are. Whether you are rich, poor, old, young, married, single, white, or black, you can have a healthy vegan life. The vegan vibes are for everyone!

Raise Your Vibe

I admit raising one's vibration can sound woo-woo, but it shouldn't. A vibration is simply how you feel and how you show up in the world. Imagine yourself on a good day. You feel light, loving, happy, and unburdened. Full of good vibes. On a bad day you feel quite the opposite: heavy, possibly unwell and unhappy, not great. Heaviness, sickness, and sadness are all lower vibration. You cannot always be happy, but your baseline can be content, light, and peaceful.

You are what you eat, so the best way to start feeling your best and raising your vibration is to eat foods that support the proper functioning of your body and mind. When you reduce or remove lower-vibration foods—foods that cause stress and inflammation in the body like highly processed food, meat, dairy, and alcohol—you start to feel better. You start to raise your vibration.

Vegan vibes are everywhere, you just have to be ready to receive them. Side effects of catching a vegan vibe include more energy, clarity of thought, greater sense of purpose, and desire to spread the vibes to others. But this is a cookbook, so let's focus on how vegan vibes taste: delicious and nourishing. They can taste like home or like a journey around the world. They can taste like comfort or like excitement and surprise. So are you ready to catch this vegan vibe?! Let's dive in.

Inspiration Everywhere

I've lived my whole life surrounded by culinary inspiration. The first inspiration came at the kitchen counter with my nana when I was a little girl. I remember the smell of her baking biscuits and frying pancakes on Sunday morning. I loved watching her peel potatoes, and wash collard greens in the sink. I can still hear the sound of her beating eggs, sugar, and butter with a hand mixer to make her famous pound cake. And my nana had the grace and patience to let me not only help her cook, but to mix my own ingredients into an inedible disaster—something she does with my own daughter every weekend at our house.

My dad was raised vegan and is an amazing cook, so I also grew up eating his delicious and fresh vegan creations. He inspired me with stories of his days working at Atlanta's OG vegan restaurant, Soul Vegetarian, in the early '80s. He would blow my mind with tales of his time as a raw vegan who would soak wild rice in water until it was tender enough to eat.

And I grew up in Atlanta, the South's most beautifully diverse city. Because my mother didn't like to cook, on any given day we'd eat handmade Mexican tamales, authentic Thai food, or Indian staples like chicken vindaloo. And then I'd go to school and hear tales of even more exotic and exciting foods from my classmates whose parents came from all around the world. I mentioned I was a picky eater—well, somehow I always made room for ethnic food! Maybe it's because most of these foods were void of the things I most disliked: steamed vegetables, dairy, red meat, and eggs.

In 2021, I returned to Atlanta after fifteen years living around the country (and a short stint abroad). Sure I've lived in New York City, Los Angeles, Boston, and Madrid. Sure I've traveled the entire globe. But the inspiration for this cookbook didn't coalesce until I came back home to my big small town, Atlanta. I realized that no matter where you live, whether it be in the largest city with the most vegan restaurants or a tiny town of fewer than one thousand people, the vegan vibes come from within. As long as you have access to fresh produce and good-quality spices, you can make the most delicious and exciting vegan food at home. And it doesn't have to be difficult or cost a lot of money.

Make It Easy

One reality about my return to Atlanta is that I came home as a single mother to my beautiful daughter, Jorji. I couldn't be happier to be creating a comfortable and safe life for her in the place where I was born, but it is far from easy. I am busy raising an energetic vegan child, running a (thankfully) successful online business, putting my health and self-care first, and being a good friend and family member. Where do I find the time to cook? My approach to food has evolved to fit my busy schedule. Meals are simpler, I rely on frozen food more often, and I meal-prep with greater purpose. I couldn't live without the Instant Pot, the food processor, and most of the recipes in this cookbook. While some of the recipes in this book require a fair amount of prep, many require the bare minimum. Even exciting and gourmet-sounding recipes—like Divinely Decadent Chocolate Pancakes (page 44), Gochujang Corn Ribs (page 79), Minimalist Mushroom Bisque (page 133), and Perfect Pea Pesto Pasta (page 185)—are actually quick and easy to make, yet delicious and interesting enough to reserve for dinner parties with fancy friends.

Some recipes in this cookbook require lots of chopping prep, but I encourage you to be like me and use a food processor or veggie chopper to do the heavy lifting. The goal is to help you eat more wholesome and delicious plant-based food so your baseline is feeling your absolute best.

The Fundamentals of Veganism

Vegans eat plants: abundant, beautiful, nutritious, delicious, and wide-ranging plants.

We eat leafy greens, beans, fruits, mushrooms, nuts, grains, spices. We even eat plant-based foods like chocolate, sugar, soda, alcohol, and bread, as long as no animal products have been added in their processing. The diversity of food that a vegan may eat is incredible and underrated. While animal foods are limited to meat, dairy, and fish, the range of edible plants is unimaginable!

No matter where you live, you will have access to an amazing variety of foods that are delicious, nourishing, and nutritious. One of my favorite vegan vibes is to think in abundance! For every animal product you stop eating, you can eat ten more plants that give you as much or more satisfaction when you know how to prepare them.

Instead of focusing on what vegans don't eat, I always like to celebrate the abundance of what we do enjoy. Think about it like this: To make animal products tasty, cooks must rely on spices that derive from plants. Why not skip the animal and replace it with a plant that has as much protein, and way more nutrients and flavor on its own?

The term *plant-based* can refer to a number of different things. If someone identifies as plant-based, that may mean they eat a diet that consists mostly of plants, or it may mean they are totally vegan. In my own recipes, I use plant-based as a synonym for vegan. However, when you're purchasing processed foods, a product labeled as plant-based may not technically be vegan. Check the ingredient label before purchasing.

Vegan Can Be Healthiest

Numerous studies have shown that the vegan diet outperforms other diets in increasing longevity and reducing your risk of suffering from the most common causes of death—heart disease, stroke, and cancer.

You can enjoy the incredible benefits of plant-based eating by prioritizing wholesome foods that are as unprocessed as possible. Think of the Mediterranean diet: It is high in vegetables, fruit, whole grains, and healthy fats. It makes no room for highly processed food. Even so, it is not as effective as a vegan diet in reducing the risk of heart disease, cancer, and diabetes.

Since the day I became vegan, my family has been incredibly supportive. My father was raised vegan, so he was already well aware of the benefits of eating this way. Actually, he taught me so much of what I know about cooking in general. He's an amazing chef. My dad isn't vegan now, but his mostly plant-based diet is certainly helpful in supporting his busy lifestyle of work, constant travel, and family obligations.

My nana and her doctors attribute her amazing health and longevity to her mostly plant-based diet as well. Since she gave up meat, her doctors have taken her off many high blood pressure medications. She lost weight, has incredible energy, and looks twenty-five years younger.

Plants have always been at the center of my mom's diet, though she still consumes dairy and fish. She stopped eating meat as a child, and taught me the importance of eating a plant-based diet long before we had that term to define it. This woman looks twenty years younger, and is in amazing health. She hikes as much as eight miles a day and has seemingly endless energy. No shade on my family members who eat a Standard American Diet, but they are certainly not doing as well as the mostly plant eaters.

Studies show that vegans on average live longer, are less likely to have chronic diseases like heart disease and diabetes, and have a lower risk for all types of cancer. We can assume that the majority of participants in all of these studies ate a lot of wholesome plants like whole grains, dark leafy veggies, legumes, and fruit, not a diet rich in Oreos (which are vegan) and other ultraprocessed food.

In the United States, and most countries, almost all animals slaughtered for meat and exploited for dairy and eggs live in hellish conditions without access to their natural diet and movement. The truth is that 99 percent of all animal protein comes from factory-farmed animals. The abysmal conditions in which animals are raised for food requires the regular use of antibiotics, growth hormones, synthetic growth enhancers, pesticides, and nutrient supplementation. Farm-raised fish—yes, even salmon—swim their whole life in pools of their own excrement. Chickens and other poultry live in such tight quarters their beaks must be trimmed to prevent them from pecking each other to death. Female pigs are confined to gestation crates barely bigger than their own bodies so that they may be conveniently impregnated over and over until they are "spent" and sent to slaughter. Dairy cows live in horrors just as bad as the pigs. The meat and dairy from these animals have more fat and fewer antioxidants than those from their grass-fed counterparts. They also contain potentially harmful growth hormones and antibiotics. In the end, the nutritional quality of almost all animal products at the grocery store is far inferior to what consumers think they are getting—meat from happy grazing cows or eggs from chickens happily living on a small farm.

Protein Myth

There is a terribly pervasive myth that vegan diets are unavoidably deficient in protein and that animal-sourced protein is of higher quality than that from plants. Made up of amino acids, protein is the building block of life. Plant life, too. There are twenty amino acids the body needs for proper functioning. Our bodies produce eleven of these amino acids, while the remaining nine must come from the food we eat. These nine are called essential amino acids. Contrary to popular belief, all plant foods contain all twenty amino acids. However, some plant foods contain suboptimal levels of some of the essential amino acids. Foods that contain optimal levels of all nine are considered complete proteins. Examples of these foods are meat, soy, eggs, dairy, nutritional yeast, hemp seeds, and quinoa.

You don't have to get the nine essential amino acids from one food item. Instead, you can eat a wide variety of plant protein to feed your body optimal amounts of all the amino acids it needs. For example, beans and rice individually are low in some essential amino acids, but together combine to create optimal levels of all the essential amino acids. There is no need to worry about combining foods with different amino acid profiles every day. When protein is consumed, the body breaks it down into its amino acid parts in order to deploy these acids throughout the body. When you eat these foods, even separately throughout the week, your body will still get the essential amino acids it requires. See my recommendations for creating The Perfect Plate (page 21).

While it is true that some plants have higher amounts of protein than others, all plants do contain protein in varying levels. It should be easy to consume enough protein while following a whole-food vegan eating protocol. Plants with the highest protein are legumes, green vegetables, nuts and seeds, and whole grains. The healthiest diet prioritizes a healthy balance of these foods along with fruit, mushrooms, and spices. Without conscious effort, you will consume plenty of protein. A good way to know if you're eating enough is to pay attention to whether or not you feel satiated and nourished after a meal. If you still feel hungry, eat more unprocessed plant-based food. Yes, as long as you feel satiated, you are getting enough protein. How much protein you need depends heavily on your size, activity level, whether or not you are pregnant, and your sex. For example, a woman who exercises a lot will need a lot more protein than a woman who does not.

Personally, I prefer to eat a lot of protein every day—80-plus grams a day. The recommendation for a woman my size and activity level is 54 grams a day, yet I find that a high-protein vegan diet gives me more energy, supports lean muscle, increases my fitness stamina, and helps me stay full for longer. I get my protein from lentils, soy (tofu, tempeh, and edamame), beans, nuts, seeds, whole grains, green veggies, and mushrooms. If I'm having a super-busy, active day I might use a plant-based protein powder in my smoothie; but I much prefer to bulk it up by adding a couple tablespoons of hemp seeds, almond butter, and flaxseed meal. And it even tastes delicious!

Americans are eating plenty of protein, and yet we suffer the highest rates of preventable chronic diseases. One reason for this is that the majority of protein in the Standard American Diet is animal derived. Americans don't eat nearly enough legumes, nuts, seeds, and vegetables. We know that vegan diets result in the lowest risk of all-cause mortality; not only are vegans *not* eating too little protein, but plant-based protein seems to have some benefits.

Let the following chart give you an understanding of how easy it is to consume ample amounts of protein on a vegan diet. A tiny bowl of oatmeal in the morning topped with walnuts contains 10 grams of protein. Later in the day you might enjoy a Kimchi Kale Salad (page 113) with a side of brown rice and easily get at least 23.2 grams of protein. For dinner you could have Teriyaki Tempeh Tacos (page 172) and a side of steamed broccoli, which would be at least 24.5 grams. Not to mention a snack— ¼ cup of sunflower seeds with some fresh fruit is perfect; that's at least 6 grams right there. By the end of the day, eating three meals and one small snack, you've consumed at least 63.7 grams of protein, and many more health-supportive nutrients like fiber, antioxidants, vitamins, and minerals.

PLANT FOOD	SERVING SIZE	PROTEIN
Lentils	1 cup cooked	18 grams
Chickpeas	1 cup cooked	14.5 grams
Rolled oats	1 cup cooked	6 grams
Brown rice	1 cup cooked	5 grams
Broccoli	1 cup steamed	2 grams
Kale	1 packed cup, steamed	3.7 grams
Walnuts	¼ cup	4 grams
Sunflower seeds	¼ cup	6 grams
Tofu	½ block (7.5 ounces/ 212 grams)	20 grams
Tempeh	½ block (3.5 ounces/ 105 grams)	22.5 grams

Fiber Is the Focus

When people ask me where I get my protein, I educate them kindly. Then I ask, "Where do you get your fiber?" Fiber isn't as sexy as protein, but it should be. This incredibly important nutrient is only available in plants and mushrooms, and is essential for gut, digestive, and heart health. While the recommended daily intake of fiber is 25 to 30 grams, the average American only eats around 15 grams a day. Diets low in fiber are linked to heart disease, colorectal cancers, diabetes, and digestive problems.

Fiber is abundant within all whole plants. I love the analogy by Dr. Michael Greger, author of How Not to Die: "Animals have bones to hold them up, but plants—and only plants—have fiber."

The human body cannot digest fiber. Instead, it utilizes the two types of fiber— soluble and insoluble. I think of it like this: Soluble fiber is the bulk, while insoluble fiber is the broom. When you are eating a wholesome vegan diet it is not too important to worry about what kind of fiber you're getting at any given meal. Instead prioritize eating a diet that is rich in fiber from all sorts of delicious plant-based food.

Though the human body cannot digest fiber, it is essential for moving food, nutrients, and waste through the system. And it is food for the incredibly important gut microbiome. The billions of good bacteria living in your gut rely on the fiber from your diet, and in turn perform myriad health-supportive functions in your body. The gut microbiome is critical for gut health, mental health, immune health, heart health, and potentially all other systems in your body. Healthy gut, healthy human. And one of the best ways to promote a healthy microbiome is to eat a diet rich in fiber. Note that processed foods, even if they are vegan, have less fiber than whole foods. Another good reason to enjoy your processed goodies in moderation.

Did you know that the bacteria in your gut have their own food cravings that affect what you crave? People who mainly eat processed foods are populated by bacteria that crave those foods; the food came first. You can change your gut cravings by changing your diet. Eat more wholesome plant-based food, and you will start to build healthy gut flora that craves even more wholesome food. That is to say, give yourself grace if you find it hard to kick cravings; you're not the only one driving this ship. But also know that you have the power to make those cravings a thing of the past.

Nutrient Deficiencies

When you eat enough wholesome vegan food to feel satiated, nourished, and energized, it is very unlikely that you will suffer from nutrient deficiencies, unless you have an underlying medical condition. The main deficiencies people worry about are protein, iron, omega-3 fatty acids, vitamin B12, and iodine. We've already addressed protein, but what about the other nutrients?

Iron is present in legumes, including beans and lentils, in high amounts. It is also found in dark leafy greens, beets, oats and other whole grains, nuts, and seeds. A healthy vegan diet is rich in these foods, so you should have no problem getting enough iron. Not only are these foods rich in iron, but some are also rich in vitamin C, an essential nutrient that helps the body metabolize the iron you consume.

Omega-3 fatty acids are, among other functions, essential for heart and cognitive health. In America we've been misled to believe that fatty fish is the only nutritionally sufficient form of omega-3s. While it is true that the most common sources of DHA and EPA omega-3 fatty acids are seafood, these forms are also found in algae (which is how it ended up in the fish to begin with). The only essential type of omega-3—meaning your body must get it from food—is ALA, which is abundant in plant foods like walnuts, dark leafy greens, flaxseed, and many other commonly eaten plants. While DHA and EPA are important, your body converts ALA into these forms of the fatty acids, which is why they are not considered essential. Still, I like to go the extra mile and take an algae-based DHA omega-3 liquid supplement. I do this because there has been some research suggesting that it may further enhance cognitive function, fetal brain development, immune health, and heart health.

Vitamin B12 is no joke and most vegans should consider taking a supplement. It's an essential nutrient needed in DNA production, nervous system function, protein metabolism, and the formation of red blood cells. It is made by bacteria; it's not made by animals. The human brain evolved to need B12, but because of poor soil health and modern cleanliness, most of us cannot get enough of this nutrient from our food anymore. Although B12 is found in animal flesh, factory-farmed animals must be given B12 supplements for it to end up in their meat.

Iodine is in more than salt. Essential for thyroid health, iodine is a trace mineral found in greatest abundance in the ocean. Iodine is present in soil, so plants do contain some, however the best plant-based dietary source is iodized sea salt and seaweed. Other sources of iodine include navy beans and prunes. Iodine deficiency is very dangerous and can lead to goiter and hypothyroidism. Avoid these issues by consuming seaweed regularly, eating a rich plant-based diet, and using iodized sea salt.

Vegan Doesn't Always Mean Healthy

As veganism becomes more mainstream, we also find more ultraprocessed vegan foods on the shelves at our local grocery stores. Though I am excited that people are swapping animal products for plant-based ones, I cannot help but regret the rise of vegan ultraprocessed foods. I occasionally enjoy highly processed food, but in strict moderation. By now we should all understand the dangers of ultraprocessed foods in the modern American diet. We have become the least-healthy rich nation in the world because of our reliance on highly processed foods. For decades Americans have been eating too many processed meats, grains, and sweets, and not nearly enough wholesome plants. Vegan ultraprocessed food, like faux meat and dairy, does save animals (amen). But does it contribute to helping Americans eat more nutrient-dense wholesome food? One thing I've learned on my health journey is that true health and healing must be holistic and seek to address the root of the problem. Humans, like all animals, are meant to eat whole food, not processed.

Eating 80/20 or 90/10

At the same time, I am not a health nut. Instead I practice, and recommend, a 90/10 way of eating. That means that at least 90 percent of the time I consume wholesome plants like vegetables, fruits, mushrooms, beans, whole grains, nuts, and seeds. I reserve highly processed or sugary foods, and alcoholic beverages, for no more than 10 percent of my diet. When I became vegan in 2011, I definitely practiced more of an 80/20 way of eating, which I still recommend, but as I age, I've mindfully reduced my consumption of processed and packaged foods to 10 percent.

An example of an 80/20 way of eating might look like eating about four less-than-healthy meals in a week of twenty-one meals. I don't keep track of my meals; I just know if I'm eating in the best way to support the thriving of my body and mind. I can feel it in my energy levels, digestion, clarity, and satiety.

Even in this cookbook you will find recipes that don't skimp on sugar and other less-than-healthy ingredients; I'm looking at you, desserts and cocktails. But when sugary sweets and alcohol make up such a small amount of your food intake, you don't suffer the effects as drastically. By focusing on wholesome foods you give your body the strength it needs to remove dietary toxins when you do indulge.

This same way of eating can help you transition to a vegan lifestyle if you haven't yet. Eat vegan (even if it's processed) 80 percent of the time, and limit animal products to 20 percent or less. Over time you will find it easier and easier to give up the animal products or replace them with plant-based alternatives. Then once you are vegan, you can transition away from the processed foods. There isn't a rule to suit everyone; each individual should use trial and error to find what is best for their body and bandwidth.

I don't usually quote insurance companies, but I can't help but love this vegan transition guide by Kaiser Permanente. They recommend the following steps to becoming vegan.

STEP ONE
Pay attention to the foods you eat that are already vegan: fruit, veggies, meals that just happen to be vegan.

STEP TWO
Make a list of foods you already love and can easily make vegan. For example, replace the ground turkey in spaghetti with a vegan ground meat alternative like lentils or Beyond Meat.

[P.S. Try my Righteous Rigatoni Bolognese (page 144).]

STEP THREE
Try new vegan recipes!

[And that's where this cookbook, my first cookbook, *Sweet Potato Soul*, and my blog come in. But I'm not the only vegan chef. There are thousands of amazing vegan cookbooks waiting to be invited into your kitchen.]

Food Journaling
Beginners may find it helpful to keep a food journal to track what they are eating. Whether you are on this journey to eat healthier or to become fully vegan, making tweaks comes easier when you have a clear view of what you're eating on a daily basis. Following a meal plan will also make it easier to stick to a vegan or plant-based diet protocol. Visit my blog, sweetpotatosoul.com, to download meal plans.

HOW TO KEEP A FOOD JOURNAL

DATE	WHAT TIME	WHAT I ATE	HOW IT MADE ME FEEL (energized, nourished, too full, still hungry, gassy, etc.)
	Breakfast		
	Lunch		
	Dinner		
	Snacks		

The Perfect Plate

The perfect plate will be beautiful, like a rainbow, with a balance of vegetables, a legume, a whole grain, and a healthy fat. Many of the entrées in this cookbook are the perfect plate in a pot. For example, the Thai Taste Tofu Stir-Fry (page 186) consists of many different vegetables (onions, peppers, red cabbage, broccoli), a healthy fat in the form of almond butter, and tofu as the legume, served over fluffy brown rice, the whole grain.

I might make the Miso Creamy Corn Pasta (page 153) more balanced by garnishing it with a generous sprinkle of parsley and serving it alongside Crispy Cranberry Brussels Sprouts (page 95). And I adore a balanced breakfast, so I love to make the Wild Morning Mushroom Avocado Toast (page 61): sourdough or whole-grain bread and healthy avocado fat, topped with herbs and mushrooms (a fair stand-in for protein-rich legumes). Even if I'm hosting Mother's Day brunch, I will make Divinely Decadent Chocolate Pancakes (page 44) with fiber-rich spelt flour, and serve them along with Leek Mushroom Quiche (page 50) for a legume-based option, and a gorgeous Naked Niçoise Salad (page 114) for a rainbow platter of veggies.

Mostly I rely on a couple of large entrées that can be enjoyed all week, and balance them with a vibrant salad or nourishing soup. For example, I'll make the Black-Eyed Pea Curry (page 169) and have it one day with a Fennel Beet Salad (page 112) and the next with a Dilly Broccoli Salad (page 121), which is so easy to make.

Meal prep will make all your vegan eating easier. If possible, take a few hours one or two days a week to make meals you can enjoy as leftovers. Stews and soups can even be frozen for later!

Animal Agriculture Is a Vibe Killer

If you are an animal lover like me, and even if you're not, you will be horrified by the realities of the animal agriculture system. Worldwide over ninety billion land animals are killed each year for food, and this number doesn't account for fish and other marine life. A staggering 99 percent of animal products come from factory farming operations, where conditions for the animals are unimaginably cruel, and employees show up to a hazardous work environment. Animal agriculture pollutes local ecosystems and is an enormous contributor to greenhouse gas emissions.

We don't have much power in this world over what happens, but we do have immense power over what we eat and how we choose to live. And what we choose to spend our money on is a vote. Life can feel disempowering, especially when you follow the news and social media cycles. There's always a war, always suffering, always injustice. You can donate money, post on social media, talk about it over the dinner table, but there is no power like the power of your individual choice. You eat three meals a day, at least. That's three votes a day, twenty-one a week.

You cannot make everyone become vegan, but you'd be amazed at the ripple effect your actions have on others. Since I became vegan in 2011, many of my friends have also become vegan, and almost all of them now eat a predominantly plant-based diet. And the effect ripples on.

Organic Produce?

Is organic food worth the higher price? It all depends on the food, your goals, and your budget. The most important thing is to eat lots of fruits and veggies, regardless of whether they are conventionally grown or organic.

It is usually less important to buy organic bananas, avocados, and oranges because these fruits have thick skin that protects the flesh inside from coming into contact with pesticides. On the other hand, studies show that pesticides may cling to thin-skinned fruits like apples and berries even after they've been washed. However, the antioxidant power in such fruits may cancel out any potential effect from the lingering pesticide.

Some studies show that organic produce may have higher levels of antioxidants and phytonutrients than their conventionally grown counterparts. But organic doesn't always mean better. There have been many times when I've visited my local grocery store and found conventionally grown local produce that looks much fresher than the organic veggies grown on the other side of the country. If you are committed to buying certain produce organic, consider purchasing it frozen. Frozen produce is flash frozen at its peak of freshness, and since freezing does not destroy nutrients, frozen fruits and veggies may be even more nutritious than that wilted produce sitting on the shelf. That said, frozen veggies won't work when you're making many of the recipes in this book, like the Kimchi Kale Salad (page 113) or Za'atar Cauliflower Steaks (page 175). Choose the produce that looks freshest whether or not it is organic.

My favorite way to guarantee the freshness and nutritional value of my fruits and vegetables is to buy them at a local farmers' market. I am blessed to live in a big city with a year-round market within walking distance of my house. Even if that's not an option for you, that doesn't mean you can't eat healthy produce grown in healthy soil. If you have no farmers' market around, consider growing your own produce at home. Even growing just one staple food like kale, collards, tomatoes, or peppers can make a positive impact on your health if it gets you to eat more veggies.

Grains like wheat and oats are heavily sprayed with glyphosate, an herbicide banned in many countries. Ever heard of Roundup, Monsanto's wonder herbicide? That is glyphosate, and it is sprayed on American-grown grains to stop weed growth. While the EPA attests that glyphosate levels in the American food system are safe, it is well known that exposure to high amounts of this chemical can cause cancer. For a few more dollars you can buy organic grains and minimize your glyphosate exposure even more. Luckily organic grains are easily accessible thanks to Costco, Trader Joe's, big-box grocery stores, and the Internet. I recommend buying organic oats, wheat products, and corn.

When it comes to legumes, I like to prioritize organic soy products. I eat a ton of soy in the form of tofu, soy milk, edamame (you've got to try the Sticky Fingers Edamame on page 97), and soy sauce. While soy is known to reduce the risk of certain types of cancer, improve heart health, and boost the body's defenses with antioxidants, it is also true that 98 percent of American-grown soy is sprayed with glyphosate. Most soy grown in the United States goes to feed livestock, not humans. And most large grocery stores carry organic soy products.

How to Use This Cookbook

Want to eat delicious, soulful, nutritious food that happens to be vegan and is easy to make?

I have the perfect cookbook for you, and you're reading it now! Whether you're a busy working mom, a domestic goddess, or a complete cooking novice, this cookbook is for you. Your approach to the recipes may be different—for example, a busy mom might follow my Cheat Code Tools (page 37) for making prep easy, while a domestic goddess may want to chop every last garlic clove by hand. Whatever the case, the recipes in this cookbook are fun, colorful, and super tasty.

If you're hungry for a fun vegan breakfast, try the Divinely Decadent Chocolate Pancakes (page 44). Rather start the day with a savory treat? Yeah, me, too. Try the incredible Wild Morning Mushroom Avocado Toast (page 61). And if it's time to host brunch, you must make room on the menu for Leek Mushroom Quiche (page 50), Bodacious Baked Banana French Toast (page 57), and Baby J's Spelt Biscuits (page 47) topped with Sweet Potato Butter (page 48). And that's just the first chapter! This cookbook is filled with soulful, happy recipes; you're sure to find many calling your name.

If you're new to vegan eating, want to cook at home more often, or just want to try a really yummy recipe, make a meal plan. I have a template you can download from my website to fill in with these and other recipes you want to try.

Always read through the recipe before you begin prepping and cooking. A quick read takes no more than two minutes, but it is one of the most important steps to following a recipe accurately. Know what you're getting yourself into before you get started, even if the recipe is easy.

When it's time to start cooking, gather your ingredients and do your prep. Another way to guarantee success is to measure out ingredients like spices, grains, beans, etc., before you begin cooking. You should also prep aromatics (onions and garlic) and veggies before turning on the stove.

Have fun. I truly believe that cooking at home should be fun and relaxing. Stressful cooking is the perfect way to lower the vibration of your meal. So take a deep breath, save the drama for your mama, prep your ingredients, and have fun cooking. I promise the meal will taste even better at the end.

Vegan Vibes Menus

A Vibey Brunch
Divinely Decadent Chocolate Pancakes
(page 44)
Lentil Lover Breakfast Sausages (page 49)
Best Ever Tofu Scramble (page 54)
Wild Morning Mushroom Avocado Toast
(page 61)
Rad Strawberry Salad (page 122)
Peach Tea Soda (page 216)

Slay the Summer Cookout
Gochujang Corn Ribs (page 79)
Peach White Bean Salad (page 117)
Watermelon Gazpacho (page 134)
Mushroom Carnitas Tacos (page 162)
Miso Caramel-y Banana Pudding (page 192)
Pineapple Rose Sangria (page 231)

Rainbow Meal Prep
Leek Mushroom Quiche (page 50)
Beta-Boost Carrot & Mango Muffins (page 67)
Magical Mushroom Hummus (page 91)
Hot Stuff Harissa Almonds (page 92)
Fennel Beet Salad (page 112)
West African Nut Stew (page 180)

Kid-Friendly Vittles
Baby J's Spelt Biscuits (page 47) with
Sweet Potato Butter (page 48)
Better Buttermilk Waffles (page 58)
Eat Mor Tofu Nuggets (page 102)
Dilly Broccoli Salad (page 121)
Righteous Rigatoni Bolognese (page 144)
Black Bean Crust Pizza (page 154)

Mindfully Missing Meat
Addictive Shiitake Bacon (page 66)
Orange Cauliflower Bites (page 100)
Seaside Stew (page 138)
Tofu Salmon (page 160)
Mushroom Bulgogi Lettuce Cups (page 176)
Lion's Mane Crab Cakes (page 178)

Impress Your Boo
Naked Niçoise Salad (page 114)
Minimalist Mushroom Bisque (page 133)
Simple Oyster Mushroom Steaks (page 183)
Perfect Pea Pesto Pasta (page 185)
No-Bake Cherry Walnut Crumble (page 209)
Strawberry Bramble (page 227)

Pantry Essentials

*This is by no means an exhaustive list
of everything I keep in my pantry.*

These are some of the most common ingredients found in this cookbook, and that I always keep stocked in my pantry.

Long Live Legumes

A fun fact: *Legume* technically refers to the pea/bean pod, while the term *pulse* refers to the peas, beans, etc. inside the pod. I typically use the term *legume* to refer to all beans, lentils, and peas. And what is the difference between a pea and a bean? Peas and beans are both pulses, though peas are usually round—like green peas and chickpeas—and often green (chickpeas are green before they are dried).

Legumes are an excellent and very inexpensive plant-based protein source. Eat them in abundance to help meet your body's requirements for protein, fiber, antioxidants, vitamins, and minerals.

Beans & Peas

At the core of a healthy diet lie legumes. A common dietary trait of people who live in blue zones—places on Earth with the longest life expectancy—is the regular consumption of beans, lentils, and peas. Researchers have found that eating legumes on a daily basis can add ten years to your life. Legumes are so delicious and versatile, why not indulge?

My pantry is stocked with a variety of dried beans. I love Camellia brand for everyday beans like black beans, chickpeas, red kidney beans, and black-eyed peas. I splurge on Rancho Gordo beans when I want to try something exotic. Beans are also available in bulk at health food stores. Buying in bulk is the most cost effective. I also stock the shelves with a variety of canned beans for when I forget to soak beans, or don't have time to wait for them to cook. Look for canned beans that are unsalted and have only two ingredients: beans and water. Whole Foods' 365 brand is my favorite low-cost canned bean option. Eden brand beans is another fantastic choice.

Lentils

Lentils have even more protein than beans, and they cook in half the time without the need for overnight soaking. Anecdotally, I've been told that lentils do not cause as much gassiness as beans do.

I love lentils for their versatility, nutritional benefits, and nutty taste. Like beans, there are many varieties of lentils. You'll always find green lentils, red lentils, French Puy lentils, and yellow split lentils in my pantry. Each has a different flavor and texture profile in recipes. Try the Lovely Lentil Sweet Potato Salad (page 118) and the Righteous Rigatoni Bolognese (page 144) to fall in love with lentils.

Beans Giving You Gas & a Tummy Ache?

If you aren't already consuming beans on a regular basis, they may cause you some gastrointestinal upset. While beans are a superior food, it is essential to prepare them properly. To help reduce the gas-causing compounds in beans, soak them in water with ½ teaspoon baking soda for 8 hours—overnight—before cooking. It is very important to cook beans thoroughly before eating. Different beans have different cook times, but you'll know the beans are done when they are tender throughout.

The oligosaccharides in beans are what causes some people to experience discomfort after consumption. However, oligosaccharides are important for healthy gut bacteria, gut health, and the immune system. Intentionally work small portions of beans into your diet to build your body's ability to process this gas-causing compound. A little Magical Mushroom Hummus (page 91) or Brilliant Beet Black Bean Dip (page 88) a day should help. As someone who has eaten beans almost every day of her life, I never get gas, bloating, or stomachaches from this superfood. If you have a lot of pain from eating beans, please speak to your doctor, as you may be intolerant of some legumes.

Soy

Incredibly versatile, soy is used to make everything from tofu and tempeh (fermented soybean cake) to soy sauce and oil. Native to East Asia, soybeans have been cultivated for thousands of years. Soybeans are a complete protein, high in fiber, and rich in minerals like iron, magnesium, and calcium. Soy also contains isoflavones, a group of phytoestrogens that may be responsible for soy's role in reducing the risk of breast and prostate cancers.

Most soy grown in the world is GMO and goes to feed livestock. Organic and non-GMO soy products are available at all grocery stores. While studies show the benefits of soy phytoestrogens in reducing the risk of breast and prostate cancers, the same cannot be said for the consumption of hormones from animal protein. Limit your exposure to animal estrogens and hormone-disrupting GMOs by reducing your consumption of animal products.

SOY MILK

I recommend buying soy milk without added sugar or flavor—organic soybeans and water should be the only ingredients. Trader Joe's brand and West Life both offer shelf-stable soy milk with just soybeans and water. You can also find fresh soy milk at Asian grocery stores. Save money and guarantee yourself the freshest soy milk by making it at home. I use soy milk in all of my vegan baking, pancake making, and savory recipes that would otherwise call for dairy milk.

MISO

Invented in Japan, miso is a versatile and nutritious paste of fermented soybeans, though other types of beans and grains can be used as well. Overall, the flavor of miso is salty and savory, but different varieties have unique flavors and colors. In this cookbook I always call for mellow (white) miso, which has a mild but delightfully umami taste. To make miso, soybeans are cooked, mashed, and inoculated with a rice koji—a mold that assists in fermenting the beans and giving it its signature flavor. The inoculated soybeans are packed tightly in a jar, and kept in a cool dark place for six months. After six months you have a delicious, beautiful miso that is bursting with rich umami flavor, nutrients, and gut beneficial probiotics. Give it a try in Collard Greens Miso Soup (page 137), Dilly Broccoli Salad (page 121), and Perfect Pea Pesto Pasta (page 185).

TOFU

Produced by curdling soy milk, tofu is one extremely versatile food. In this cookbook you'll find tofu in place of eggs in the nutritious Best Ever Tofu Scramble (page 54), used to make the savory Leek Mushroom Quiche (page 50), air-fried into nuggets (page 102) à la Chick-fil-A, and transformed into Tofu Salmon (page 160). Tofu is rich in protein and calcium—one serving provides as much as a glass of milk.

My recipes call for extra-firm tofu or firm tofu, which can be found in most grocery stores. Tofu is a staple ingredient in many East Asian cuisines, and the types found in this cookbook are merely two of the various varieties found throughout Asia, and especially Japan.

TEMPEH

One of my favorite foods, tempeh, is a fermented soybean cake. Tempeh is far less processed than tofu, because it is made with whole soybeans. To make it, cooked soybeans are inoculated with a fungus spore, and allowed to ferment for a few days. The end result is a nutritious food that is easy to digest, is full of probiotics, and has a meaty texture. Sometimes soybeans are mixed with whole grains, like brown rice, to make tempeh. You can also find soy-free tempeh made from other legumes and grains, or you can make your own at home. It's surprisingly easy!

This delicious soy product was invented in Indonesia, and for hundreds of years has served as a staple food product, like tofu has in East Asia.

Tempeh is a great source of fiber, iron, magnesium, vitamin B6, potassium, and calcium. It is also rich in protein: Just 1 cup contains 31 grams of protein.

Spectacular Seeds & Nuts

A tiny pumpkin seed has the potential to grow into an enormous pumpkin, so imagine how much nutrition that seed must contain. Turns out the same nutrition packed in that little seed can be unleashed inside you when you eat it. It's no wonder studies show that eating more nuts and seeds can add years to your life. Note: You will not grow a pumpkin inside your stomach when you eat pumpkin seeds. :)

Stock your pantry with a wide variety of nuts and seeds that you can snack on throughout the day, add to recipes, and blend into smoothies. Nuts and seeds can be expensive, so consider purchasing them in bulk at a health food store. I find that Costco has the best prices on nuts. Keep in mind, though, that nuts have a shelf life, so if you purchase them in bulk, store them in the freezer to keep them fresh longer.

Nuts and seeds are a terrific source of plant-based protein, healthy fats, omega-3 fatty acids, minerals, vitamins, and antioxidants.

You'll find plenty of delicious nut and seed recipes in this cookbook, like the Sunflower Cheese (page 84), Hot Stuff Harissa Almonds (page 92), Curry Crunch Pepitas (page 94), and Walnut Parmesan (page 236).

Magical Mushrooms

Mushrooms truly are magical, and I'm not referring to the psychedelic ones. Mushrooms are the fruiting body of a fungus. That's right, mushrooms are not plants. There are thousands of different types of mushrooms, some of which are toxic to humans, and some less than tasty, but we'll focus on the delicious culinary mushrooms found in this cookbook. There are hundreds of culinary mushrooms, but in this cookbook you'll encounter Baby Bella (aka cremini), oyster, king oyster or trumpet, shiitake, and lion's mane—and even porcini mushroom powder.

Benefits of Mushrooms

Culinary mushrooms are nutritious, versatile, flavorful, easy to cook, and a terrific replacement for meat. Studies have linked mushrooms to a lower risk of cancer, improved gut health, brain health, and low cholesterol. Though they aren't plants, mushrooms are a good source of dietary fiber and are a complete protein, meaning they contain all nine essential amino acids. Per gram mushrooms aren't as protein-rich as legumes, but you shouldn't let that stop you from eating them regularly.

Where Can I Find Them?

Of the mushrooms used in this cookbook, the easiest to find will be cremini (Baby Bellas) as they are readily available at most local grocery stores. But you may need to head to your local

Asian or international grocery store for the best-quality (and best-priced) oyster, king oyster, lion's mane, and shiitake mushrooms. You may also find these mushrooms at your local farmers' market if you have one. These mushrooms can also be grown at home with a kit and the right conditions.

Cooking Tips

Mushrooms are so inherently flavorful that they are often used as a spice for meat and blander foods. Porcini and truffle mushroom powders are some of my favorite ingredients! Because they are so flavorful, mushrooms do not need to be cooked with a lot of spice to be delicious. One of my favorite ways to cook a mushroom is detailed in the Simple Oyster Mushroom Steaks (page 183), in which pan-seared mushrooms are seasoned with fresh garlic and salt for a truly sublime dish. To enhance a mushroom's meatiness, place a heavy lid, bacon press, or cast-iron skillet directly on top of the mushroom as it cooks—about 20 minutes, depending on the mushroom. This pressure concentrates the flavor and fibers, resulting in a rich and savory meat replacement.

Always cook mushrooms before eating, as most—even raw white mushrooms—contain a toxin called agaritine that is destroyed with cooking.

Each type of mushroom has a distinct flavor and texture, so don't assume you don't like them based on an experience with one mushroom. Don't knock them before you try the Mushroom Carnitas Tacos (page 162), made with shredded king oyster mushrooms, or the Addictive Shiitake Bacon (page 66)—my daughter Baby J's favorite way to eat them.

Powders & Spices: Flavor Enhancers

Open my spice drawers and you will be greeted with an extraordinarily messy abundance of spices. It would take me a whole book to detail the joys of each spice, so I'll shout out a few that you'll see repeatedly in this cookbook.

Garlic Powder

I use garlic powder so often I've resorted to buying it in bulk. Not only do I save money, but I rarely run out of this beloved spice. Garlic powder is dehydrated garlic ground to a grainy powder, like the texture of sand. It has a milder, less pungent flavor than fresh garlic, but does wonders to add depth and warmth to a meal. I especially like using garlic powder on roasted veggies and potatoes (try the Red Roasted Potatoes on page 98).

Smoked Paprika

My all-time favorite savory spice is probably smoked paprika. Like garlic powder, I buy it in bulk, I love it so much. Smoked paprika has a deeply smoky and savory taste, and pairs well with garlic powder and umami-rich ingredients like soy sauce and tomato paste. Most smoked paprika is "sweet," meaning it has no spiciness; however, you can buy smoked paprika with a hot punch. Plain paprika is not a replacement for smoked paprika.

Porcini Mushroom Powder

Mushroom powder offers the rich umami essence of mushrooms in a convenient powder. I use porcini mushroom powder in most of my recipes that call for this ingredient, like the Magical Mushroom Hummus (page 91) and Good & Dirty Rice (page 165). Porcini mushroom powder isn't always available at the store. I purchase it online, and it lasts a long time. Alternatively, you could grind dried porcini mushrooms—common in health food stores—to a powder in a spice grinder for the same thing.

When I want to get real fancy, I use truffle mushroom powder, which has an almost indescribable earthy flavor. Sprinkle truffle mushroom powder over avocado toast, popcorn, and soups. A little goes a very long way. Trader Joe's sells truffle mushroom powder at a low price.

Better Than Bouillon Paste

Replace cartons of vegetable broth with organic vegetable Better Than Bouillon paste. It's a better bang for your buck than veggie broth and bouillon cubes. Plus I love how it enhances soups, sauces, and stews with great, savory flavor. Because it is a paste rather than a dense bouillon cube, Better Than Bouillon dissolves easily. Find Better Than Bouillon paste at your local grocery store, at Costco, and online.

Salts

Not all salt is created equal. There are meaningful differences in sodium content, coarseness of crystals, processing, and sourcing location. I try to keep it simple.

Kosher Salt

I use kosher salt for seasoning soups and salting boiling water. I reserve this coarse salt for cooking, not for finishing.

Sea Salt

My choice of salt for sautéing veggies is sea salt, specifically Redmond Real Salt and Selina Celtic Sea Salt. I also use sea salt as a table salt.

Iodized Salt

You'll also find iodized sea salt in my kitchen. I don't use it as often as these other types of salt, but occasionally I will reach for it in place of kosher salt for salting water to boil, or sea salt for sautéing veggies. This is because iodine, an essential nutrient for thyroid function, is not found in all plants. Iodine is especially abundant in oceans, so eating a diet with plenty of seaweed will provide the body with sufficient iodine without the need for iodized salt. I just don't eat seaweed regularly. Iodized salt is table salt enriched with iodine, and as a table salt it is quite salty.

Flaky Salt

Maldon salt is a must for adding the finishing touch to meals and desserts. This delicate and flaky salt is delightfully crunchy, and less salty than table salt. Look for it at specialty grocery stores, Whole Foods, and online.

Black Salt

Black salt, or kala namak, is a must-have ingredient for making tofu scramble. Harvested from sulfur-rich salt lakes in northern India, it has an egg-like taste and funky sulfur smell. In Indian cuisines, it is often used in chutneys and chaats, and even fruit. Buy this stinky, yet essential salt at a local Indian grocery store or online. In stores it will usually be labeled kala namak.

Vinegars
Apple Cider Vinegar

I use apple cider vinegar on a daily basis for everything from baking to salad dressings. This versatile vinegar has a subtle sweetness and tons of tang. I usually reserve apple cider vinegar for cooking, but it can also be used all around the house for cleaning, and in the bathroom for hair and skin beauty treatments.

Ume Plum Vinegar

Ume plum vinegar is one of my top ten favorite ingredients. Ume fruit, sort of a cross between an apricot and a plum, can be found all over Japan. The brine used to pickle the ume is known in Japan as ume su, and in this country as ume plum vinegar. Ever since I transitioned to vegan living, it's been a staple in my pantry.

The pickling liquid used to process the ume is extremely briny, which makes it a perfect vinegar for seafood dishes, and anything that could benefit from that salty, sea-like flavor. This tangy, slightly floral, ruby red vinegar is delicious sprinkled over cooked vegetables—especially members of the cabbage family. I call for ume vinegar in a number of my recipes, such as Lion's Mane Crab Cakes (page 178) and Tofu Salmon (page 160), but it also adds zing to salad dressings and dips, and is great for making other pickled or preserved foods.

Red Wine Vinegar & Balsamic Vinegar

While I don't use these vinegars as often as I do apple cider vinegar, they are important in my pantry for their characteristic flavors. All vinegars have distinct flavors, so they cannot be used interchangeably without drastically changing the taste of a recipe. Red wine vinegar has a mild flavor and is great in salad dressings. Balsamic vinegar has a robust flavor that I especially love in dips, like the Brilliant Beet Black Bean Dip (page 88).

Go With the Grains
Brown Rice

We eat a lot of rice in my family. I choose brown rice over white because it is the whole-food version of the rice grain. Brown rice has more fiber, protein, and nutrients than white rice, which is stripped of its bran and hull and then enriched with vitamins before it is packaged. Follow my simple brown rice recipe (page 237) for perfectly fluffy rice.

Spelt Flour

You'll notice that I use spelt flour in much of my baking. Spelt, a cousin of wheat, is an ancient grain with more nutritional value than wheat. Many find that they have an easier time digesting spelt flour; this may be because it has less gluten than wheat flour and is typically not enriched with artificially derived vitamins before sale. Spelt is a great replacement for all-purpose flour in many recipes. It is only slightly denser than all-purpose flour, and it has a darker hue.

Pasta & Noodles

It is true, vegans love pasta; but who doesn't? I find myself eating more pasta and noodles these days because it is such a kid-friendly food. If my daughter, Jorji, could have it her way, we'd eat pasta or noodles every day of the week. To boost the nutrition, I like to serve pasta and noodles with a nutritious sauce like the one for Righteous Rigatoni Bolognese (page 144) made with superfood lentils, or the Perfect Pea Pesto Pasta (page 185) loaded with basil and peas. Most dried pasta is vegan, but fresh pasta is usually made with eggs. You can always use gluten-free pasta in my recipes.

Super Sauces
Mustard

I love mustard so much, I buy it in bulk at Costco. Dijon mustard is my favorite for its sharp, pungent taste and it's a key ingredient in all of my vinaigrette recipes. However, you can use yellow or brown mustard in a pinch. Yellow mustard has a milder flavor than Dijon, while brown mustard is even bolder.

Mustard seeds are packed with antioxidant and anti-inflammatory compounds, making mustard an incredibly nutritious condiment.

Tahini

Similar to peanut or almond butter, tahini is an exceptional seed butter made from sesame seeds. Its taste reminds me vaguely of peanut butter, but with a milder flavor. Tahini is integral to Middle Eastern cuisine, where it is an essential component of hummus and many other dishes. When you shake a container of tahini, it should be nice and smooth throughout. Stir the tahini with a spoon, and if you can reach the bottom of the container—rather than a brick of solid tahini—you've got yourself a great batch. Try tahini in one of the recipes in this cookbook, like Za'atar Cauliflower Steaks (page 175), Magical Mushroom Hummus (page 91), or the smooth-as-ever Tantalizing Tahini Chocolate Sauce (page 241).

Almond Butter

Almond butter can be used in savory meals as well as sweet. The best almond butter is made with only one ingredient: roasted almonds. I buy it at Costco, but if you cannot find plain unsweetened and unsalted almond butter, make your own at home. To make almond butter simply dry-roast almonds—as many as you'd like—in the oven at 325°F until fragrant and deeper brown, 15 to 20 minutes. Place the almonds in a food processor and blend until creamy, about 10 minutes. You may need to scrape the sides once or twice as it blends.

Pomegranate Molasses

Tangy, sweet, and rich, pomegranate molasses is a must-have ingredient in my kitchen. I love using it in dressings, like the pomegranate vinaigrette used in the Lovely Lentil Sweet Potato Salad (page 118). It is also delightful drizzled over fruit salads, and anywhere you want a tangy kick.

Hot Sauce

Hot sauce is vegan, y'all, so keep indulging. Because my daughter doesn't love spicy food, I rely more on hot sauce these days. I love a mild hot sauce that adds a balanced kick to my meal without covering it up in heat.

Oils

An oil's smoke point, the temperature at which it will begin to smoke, helps determine what it is best used for. For example, any oil with a smoke point of 375°F or lower should not be used for deep-frying. When heated above its smoke point, an oil may start to produce harmful compounds.

Cold-Pressed Extra-Virgin Olive Oil

Extra-virgin olive oil is my favorite type of oil for salad dressings, sautéing, and roasting. I love the characteristic olive oil flavor it gives to dressings and vegetables. Extra-virgin olive oil has a smoke point of around 400°F.

Avocado Oil

Avocado oil is my favorite neutral-tasting oil. Made from pressed avocado seeds, this oil has a smoke point of 520°F. It can be used in place of olive oil in any recipe, even dressings, but it does not have as strong a taste as olive oil does.

Unrefined Coconut Oil

Coconut oil is a great replacement for vegan butter in cooking and baking. However, it is important to remember that coconut oil has a distinctive taste. Sometimes I want that taste in a recipe, other times I don't. Coconut oil has a smoke point of 350°F and is great for baking, sautéing, and roasting.

Toasted Sesame Oil

Next to extra-virgin olive oil, sesame oil is my favorite oil for taste. It has a nutty toasted flavor and pairs well with all vegetables. It is a delicious and necessary component of the Sticky Fingers Edamame (page 97). Sesame oil has a smoke point of 350°F.

Cheat Code Tools

Kitchen Tools for Maximum Vegan Vibes

Having the right kitchen tools will make your life in the kitchen easier and more fun. In this section, you will find a list of my top picks. I recommend HomeGoods, T.J.Maxx, and Marshalls for all of your cookware—they sell a wide range of high-quality products at great prices. I rely on my local kitchen store, Cook's Warehouse, for small items like biscuit cutters and dishes. And I love Amazon for all of my small kitchen appliances—they even sell refurbished and open-box appliances at a discount.

1. Quality Pots
ENAMELED CAST-IRON SKILLET

Enameled cast-iron skillets are nonstick and won't rust like your grandma's cast-iron does. Use them for sautéing, pan-frying, making pancakes, and even baking. I recommend a 10-inch skillet.

STAINLESS STEEL SAUCEPAN

Saucepans are needed for making sauce, steaming veggies, boiling water for tea, etc. Stainless steel will last a lifetime. I have a few small to medium saucepans. If I were to purchase just one, I'd start with a 3-quart saucepan.

ENAMELED CAST-IRON DUTCH OVEN

An enameled cast-iron Dutch oven is all you need for making soups, stews, greens, baked beans, and bread. This heavy pot distributes heat evenly and can be used in the oven. Keep in mind they are very heavy. Enameled Dutch ovens come in a variety of pretty colors, which is great, because there's no way I'm moving this thing up and down to store it in a cabinet. I store my main Dutch oven right on the stove. I recommend a 5- to 7-quart Dutch oven for most recipes.

If you would rather not lift a 10-pound pot, use a stainless steel pot instead. It can also be used in the oven, and will last just as long—a lifetime.

2. Good Knives

You need an 8-inch chef's knife for everyday chopping and a paring knife for intricate slicing—for example, cutting the white pith from a bell pepper. I recommend a bread knife for cutting bread, but it is also my favorite knife for slicing tomatoes and cutting watermelon.

It is essential to keep your knives sharpened, as dull knives can easily slip, and you may chop more than a veggie. Many kitchen supply stores and farmers' markets offer knife sharpening for less than $10 per knife.

Notice I only recommended three knives. That's literally all you need.

3. Cutting Boards

One cutting board for the veggies and another for the fruit (so that it doesn't end up tasting like garlic and onions). That is all you need; but if you're like me, you'll still end up with ten-plus cutting boards that you rarely ever use. I like wooden cutting boards because they don't hold flavors and scents, and because they last a long time. Always hand-wash and dry your wooden cutting board after use; soaking it in water will prematurely age it.

Plastic cutting boards are fine. Avoid stone, glass, and cheese boards, which are more for decorative purposes.

4. Wooden Spoons

Wooden spoons are best in the kitchen. They won't scrape the enamel on your pretty pots and nonstick pans, they won't hold flavors and scents, and they have natural properties that help eliminate germs and bacteria. The only downside: Wooden spoons must be washed by hand.

5. Pancake Spatula or Turner

When I first started cooking, I didn't have a reliable pancake spatula. Flipping pancakes made me so anxious because there was always a 50 percent chance I couldn't successfully lift them from the pan. If this plight sounds familiar, get you a pancake spatula—also known as a pancake turner.

6. Good Vegetable Peeler

My nana always peels her potatoes by hand with a paring knife. That's the cool way to do it. But it does require a bit of skill. I like a simple swivel peeler. Some folks prefer a Y-peeler. Use whichever one you like best.

7. Food Processor

I highly encourage any home cook to own a food processor. The tool is the epitome of convenience, and cuts the time and energy usually associated with shredding, chopping, and mincing vegetables. It's an especially great tool to have when you're making a large quantity of something—such as a comforting stew—and need to chop a lot of ingredients. A food processor is also a game changer when making hummus, pesto, dips, raw desserts, and crumbles. Both for safety and longevity, I suggest investing a bit more in a good quality food processor, and personally love my Cuisinart 13-cup, which I've had for years and years. It comes with an assortment of attachments to conquer almost any task.

8. Instant Pot Electric Pressure Cooker

I love, and I mean love, the revolutionary invention that is the Instant Pot. Chinese Canadian businessman Robert Wang created the first iteration of this genius tool in 2010, and it has changed the lives of chefs and home cooks around the world. The Instant Pot is a must for busy home cooks because, like a stovetop pressure cooker, it cuts cooking time significantly. Instant Pots are much safer than stovetop pressure cookers, and liberate you from slaving over the hot stove for hours. You can sauté, pressure cook, steam, and ferment foods in this mechanical wizard. You can even buy an air-fryer attachment for it!

9. Air Fryer

I love the air fryer because you can crisp up food much faster, and use much less oil than you'd use in a traditional deep-fryer. You can use it in place of an oven to roast vegetables, cook sweet potato fries, and crisp up tofu nuggets and homemade granola. During the summer, when it's really hot and you don't want to heat up your entire kitchen, you can use the air fryer to make baked goods. Today, there are air-fryer toaster ovens, which I think is a great investment if you're in need of both, and don't want to use up valuable kitchen space.

10. Immersion Blender

You'll notice that I didn't include a blender on this list of kitchen essentials. I love my blenders—I have two—but if I had to choose between a blender and an immersion blender, I would go for the handheld device. An immersion blender is a handheld tool that can be immersed directly into a liquid to puree soups, blend smoothies, and create silky sauces. I recommend a rechargeable cordless immersion blender, as cords tend to get in the way, potentially knocking over ingredients and becoming a safety hazard around the stove.

BRILLIANT BREAKFASTS

Besides oatmeal, what do vegans eat for breakfast? It's a question I get all the time. While I do enjoy a hearty bowl of oatmeal, I for one can't imagine eating it every day for the rest of my long life. Thankfully there are infinite options a vegan eater can enjoy for breakfast. From savory to sweet, I share sixteen of my favorite recipes to help you break your fast in the most delicious way possible. Some are fancy and perfect for Sunday brunch, others highly nutritious and ideal for weekly meal prep.

Americans love a sweet breakfast. Waffles and pancakes are essential for lazy weekends and Sunday brunch. But starting your day with sugary sweets can have impacts on your health down the line. Moderation is key. The best everyday breakfast is rich in protein and fiber. I recommend the Leek Mushroom Quiche (page 50), Cozy Apple Spice Pancakes (page 53), Best Ever Tofu Scramble (page 54), Wild Morning Mushroom Avocado Toast (page 61), or Savory Oats Breakfast Bowls (page 65) for the most nutritious breakfast.

My family and I indulge in the Divinely Decadent Chocolate Pancakes (page 44) and Better Buttermilk Waffles (page 58) on weekends, but even then I try to pair these traditional American-style dishes with healthy sides like fresh fruit and Lentil Lover Breakfast Sausages (page 49). Gotta keep the vibes high!

Divinely Decadent
CHOCOLATE PANCAKES

Pancakes so delicious and decadent you can have them for dessert? Yes, please! These aren't your hippy great-aunt's vegan pancakes. They're made with cocoa powder and chocolate chips because you deserve to wake up to chocolate. Just make sure to buy vegan chocolate chips. I always go for dark or semisweet chocolate chunks, but use whatever you prefer. These pancakes are so sweet and decadent on their own you can skip the maple syrup. Top with fruit and vegan whipped cream instead.

These pancakes reheat well. Store extra pancakes in the refrigerator and warm them in the microwave or toaster oven for repeat joy.

MAKES 6 PANCAKES

1½ cups spelt flour or 1¼ cups all-purpose flour

¼ cup Dutch-process cocoa powder

¼ cup cane sugar

2 teaspoons baking powder

¼ teaspoon sea salt

1¼ cups plain unsweetened soy milk or other nondairy milk

1 tablespoon apple cider vinegar or distilled white vinegar

2 tablespoons extra-virgin olive oil or avocado oil

1 teaspoon pure vanilla extract

½ cup vegan chocolate chips or chunks

Vegan stick butter, for frying

Bananas and fresh berries (optional), chopped, for serving

Vegan whipped cream, for serving

1. Sift the spelt flour and cocoa powder into a large bowl. Add the cane sugar, baking powder, and salt and whisk to combine.

2. In a small bowl, combine the soy milk, vinegar, oil, and vanilla and whisk well. Pour the wet ingredients into the flour mixture and gently whisk the wet and dry until they are just combined. Using a whisk, gently fold the chocolate chips into the pancake batter.

3. In a large skillet, melt about 2 tablespoons vegan butter over medium heat and use a spatula to spread it evenly over the entire surface.

4. Spoon about ¼ cup of the pancake batter onto the hot skillet. Fit as many pancakes as you can into the skillet while maintaining at least 1 inch between the pancakes. Flip once bubbles start to emerge from the pancake center. Cook each side for about 3 minutes. Repeat with the remaining pancake batter and more butter.

5. Serve the chocolate pancakes with fruit (if using) and vegan whipped cream.

Baby J's Spelt BISCUITS

My daughter, Jorji, and I love making breakfast together. Most days it's simple oatmeal or avocado toast, but our favorite morning treat to make together are these fluffy spelt biscuits. Unlike most baking, biscuit measurements are forgiving, which is why I don't stress when making them with a little kid. Use vegan butter sticks, not tub-style vegan butter, for these biscuits. Serve them with the Sweet Potato Butter and drizzle with the Sweet Potato Syrup (page 238) for an extra-special treat.

MAKES 6 BISCUITS

Softened vegan stick butter or spray oil, for the pan

¾ cup cold plain unsweetened soy milk or other nondairy milk

1 tablespoon apple cider vinegar or distilled white vinegar

2 cups spelt flour, plus more for dusting

1 tablespoon baking powder

1½ tablespoons cane sugar

½ teaspoon sea salt

6 tablespoons cold vegan stick butter, cut into small cubes

Sweet Potato Butter (recipe follows), for serving

1. Preheat the oven to 450°F. Grease a 10-inch cast-iron skillet or 9 × 13-inch baking dish with vegan butter.

2. In a small bowl, combine the soy milk and vinegar. Let it sit and curdle while you work on the other ingredients.

3. Sift the spelt flour into a large bowl. Then whisk in the baking powder, sugar, and salt. Add the vegan butter to the bowl of flour and use a pastry cutter to combine the flour and fat (see Note, page 203). Keep cutting the dough until it's the size of tiny pebbles, reminiscent of wet grainy sand.

4. Pour the soy milk/vinegar mixture into the dough and use a wooden spoon to combine the wet and dry.

5. Generously flour a clean work surface. Transfer the dough to the floured work surface. The dough will be fairly sticky, so use the flour on the counter to help make it more manageable. Fold the dough about ten times, then pat the dough to ¾ to 1 inch thick.

6. Use a 2¾-inch biscuit cutter to cut the dough into biscuits and transfer them to the greased skillet. Leave about ½ inch of space between the biscuits. They'll expand and touch as they bake. Gather any dough scraps, pat them out, and cut to make one more biscuit. You can also shape the very last of the scraps into a biscuit and bake with the rest.

7. Bake for 12 minutes. Allow the biscuits to cool in the pan for 5 to 10 minutes before serving with sweet potato butter.

SWEET POTATO BUTTER

One of my favorite recipes to date. I am obsessed with the comforting taste of this rich sweet potato butter. You can make it a couple of ways: with a plain baked sweet potato or mashed sweet potato left over from making the Sweet Potato Syrup. I must admit the second option is even more decadent, but both are delicious.

MAKES 1 CUP

½ cup mashed sweet potato

4 tablespoons vegan stick butter, at room temperature

2 tablespoons pure maple syrup

1 teaspoon Sweet Potato Pie Spice (page 237) or pumpkin pie spice

1 teaspoon pure vanilla extract

In a food processor, combine the sweet potato, butter, maple syrup, pie spice, and vanilla and blend until creamy and smooth. Store in a glass jar in the refrigerator for up to 1 week.

DECADENT SWEET POTATO BUTTER:

Use ½ cup mashed sweet potato from the Sweet Potato Syrup (page 238). Cut the maple syrup back to 1 tablespoon and the pie spice back to ½ teaspoon.

Lentil Lover BREAKFAST SAUSAGES

The magic of lentils shines so bright in these breakfast sausages. It may seem like a lot of ingredients, but you likely have most of what you need in your pantry. You want these to be really well seasoned so you can start your day off on the right foot. I suggest adding them to the Best Ever Tofu Scramble (page 54).

MAKES 8 SAUSAGES

1 cup cooked lentils

½ teaspoon Better Than Bouillon vegetable base

¾ cup vital wheat gluten

2 tablespoons nutritional yeast

1 tablespoon potato starch

2 tablespoons pure maple syrup

1½ tablespoons soy sauce

2 tablespoons extra-virgin olive oil

1 tablespoon mellow (white) miso

2 teaspoons smoked paprika

1 teaspoon fennel seeds

1 teaspoon dried oregano

½ teaspoon freshly ground black pepper

¼ cup minced yellow or white onion

1. Place the lentils in a large bowl and mash with a fork until mostly creamy. In a measuring cup, stir together the bouillon base and ¼ cup water. Add the wheat gluten, nutritional yeast, potato starch, bouillon, maple syrup, soy sauce, 1 tablespoon of the olive oil, miso, smoked paprika, fennel, oregano, pepper, and onion to the bowl and stir until they are well combined. Use your hands to form the mixture into a tight ball.

2. Place the ball of sausage mixture on a cutting board and cut it into 8 equal portions. Use your hands to form each section into a sausage shape. Make sure to pack the mixture tightly as you shape it. Wrap each sausage tightly in a sheet of aluminum foil, twisting the ends to seal the sausage inside.

3. Set up a steamer: a basket, insert, or rack and a pot for the water. Add 1 to 2 inches of water to the pot (but not enough to touch the basket). Cover and bring the water to a boil. Add the sausages, tightly cover the pot, and steam for 40 minutes. Replenish the water if needed.

4. Remove the sausages from the heat and let cool until safe to handle. Place them, still wrapped in foil, in the refrigerator to firm up for at least 3 hours or overnight.

5. To serve, sauté the sausages, whole or sliced, in the remaining 1 tablespoon of oil in a skillet over medium heat. Cook until the edges begin to brown and crisp, about 4 minutes, flipping halfway through.

Leek Mushroom QUICHE

When I was a kid, my mom loved quiche. As someone who never loved cheese, I hated it. But I'm proud to say this vegan quiche is a hit with both my mom and me. Leek mushroom quiche has become my go-to for when I'm hosting brunch and doing weekly meal prep. If you want it extra cheesy, feel free to stir in 1 cup of your favorite meltable store-bought vegan cheese to the filling before it bakes.

SERVES 4

Flaky Pie Dough (page 208)

2 tablespoons extra-virgin olive oil

3 large leeks (well washed), white parts only, thinly sliced

4 garlic cloves, minced

1 teaspoon sea salt, plus more to taste

1½ cups thinly sliced Baby Bella or other mushrooms

1 cup marinated artichoke hearts, halved

2 tablespoons chopped oil-packed or dry-packed sun-dried tomatoes

1 teaspoon Italian seasoning

½ teaspoon fennel seeds

½ teaspoon red chili flakes

1 teaspoon freshly ground black pepper

1 (14-ounce) block firm tofu

3 tablespoons nutritional yeast

1 teaspoon apple cider vinegar or fresh lemon juice

1. Make and chill the pie dough as directed. When ready to bake, set the dough out at room temperature for 10 minutes before rolling out.

2. Preheat the oven to 375°F.

3. In a skillet, heat the oil over medium-high heat. Add the leeks, garlic, and ½ teaspoon of the sea salt. Cook until translucent, about 3 minutes.

4. Add the mushrooms and sauté until tender, about 8 minutes. Remove from the heat and stir in the artichoke hearts, sun-dried tomatoes, Italian seasoning, fennel seeds, chili flakes, and ½ teaspoon of the black pepper. Season to taste with sea salt.

5. While you are sautéing the veggies (or after), you can work on the tofu filling. In a food processor, combine the tofu, nutritional yeast, vinegar, ½ teaspoon salt, and the remaining ½ teaspoon pepper and blend until smooth.

6. Spoon the tofu mixture into the cooked veggies and stir to combine.

7. Place the ball of dough on a flour-dusted smooth stone surface (if you don't have a stone surface, use parchment paper). Use a floured rolling pin to roll the dough to ⅛ inch thick and 12 inches in diameter. Fit the dough into a 9-inch pie dish. Trim the dough to a scant 1 inch of overhang and use your fingers to crimp the edges.

8. Pour the tofu and veggie mixture into the pie shell and spread evenly.

9. Bake until the entire surface of the tofu filling is golden, especially at the center, about 40 minutes.

10. Allow it to cool for 10 to 15 minutes before serving.

Cozy Apple Spice PANCAKES

My daughter, Jorji, is the president of the pancake fan club AND the apple fan club. She would eat pancakes at every meal if I'd let her. So imagine her elation when I first served her these apple spice pancakes! Little did she know, or care, that these wholesome vegan pancakes are made with spelt and teff flour. I'm especially fond of teff for its nutty flavor, and its richness in protein, fiber, and zinc.

MAKES 8 PANCAKES

1 cup spelt flour

½ cup teff flour or buckwheat flour

2 tablespoons cane sugar

2 tablespoons light brown sugar or coconut sugar

2 teaspoons baking powder

1 teaspoon ground cinnamon

½ teaspoon sea salt

¼ teaspoon freshly grated nutmeg

Scant ⅛ teaspoon ground cloves

1 cup plain unsweetened soy milk or other nondairy milk

¼ cup plus 2 tablespoons applesauce

2 tablespoons avocado oil or extra-virgin olive oil

1 tablespoon apple cider vinegar or distilled white vinegar

1 teaspoon pure vanilla extract

Vegan stick butter, for frying

Pure maple syrup, for serving

Chopped nuts, for serving

Fresh fruit, for serving

1. Sift the spelt flour into a large bowl, then add the teff flour, cane sugar, brown sugar, baking powder, cinnamon, salt, nutmeg, and cloves. Whisk to combine.

2. In a medium bowl, combine the soy milk, applesauce, oil, vinegar, and vanilla. Stir well, then pour the wet ingredients into the flour mixture. Whisk to combine the ingredients, being careful not to overmix.

3. In a skillet, melt about 1 tablespoon vegan butter over medium heat. Add the pancake batter to the pan—about ¼ cup of batter for each pancake. Maintain at least 1 inch of space between the pancakes as they cook. Flip the pancakes once bubbles start to emerge from the center. Cook each side for about 3 minutes. Repeat with the remaining batter and more butter.

4. Serve the pancakes with maple syrup, chopped nuts, and chopped fruit.

Best Ever
TOFU SCRAMBLE

I could eat tofu scramble every day. It's filling, easy to make, nutritious, a great vessel for veggies first thing in the morning, and it pairs well with lots of other breakfast foods—I'm looking at you, avocado toast. This is the best tofu scramble because it is loaded with savory veggies and breakfast sausages. Make it in the morning, and expect to crave more throughout the day.

I recommend making your own breakfast sausages for this scramble (see Lentil Lover Breakfast Sausages, page 49), but to save time, my favorite store-bought brands of vegan sausages are Beyond Meat and Field Roast. You can also check out the two recipes I have for homemade sausages in my first cookbook, *Sweet Potato Soul*.

SERVES 6

2 tablespoons extra-virgin olive oil

½ large yellow onion, diced

3 garlic cloves, minced

1 red bell pepper, diced

3 large handfuls (about 1 pound) mushrooms, such as shiitake, oyster, or cremini, thinly sliced

6 vegan breakfast sausages, store-bought or homemade (page 49), chopped

2 (14-ounce) blocks firm tofu, pressed for at least 10 minutes

3 tablespoons nutritional yeast, plus more to taste

1 teaspoon kala namak (black salt)

½ teaspoon ground turmeric

½ to 1 teaspoon red chili flakes, to taste

1 cup frozen spinach or 4 cups chopped fresh spinach

Sea salt and freshly ground black pepper

1. In a large skillet, heat the olive oil over medium-high heat. Add the onion, garlic, and bell pepper and cook until the onions turn translucent, about 3 minutes. Add the mushrooms, stir well, and cook until they are tender and meaty, about 10 minutes. Add the sausage and cook for another 5 minutes.

2. To create a scrambled egg texture, with clean hands, crush the tofu blocks right into the skillet. (Alternatively, use a fork to mash and scramble the tofu before adding it to the skillet.)

3. Add the nutritional yeast, kala namak, turmeric, and chili flakes and stir well. Add the spinach and stir again. Cook over medium-high heat until the tofu dries out more and starts to brown at the bottom of the skillet, 5 to 10 minutes. Stir often and be careful not to let it burn.

4. Season to taste with salt and pepper and more nutritional yeast.

TO PRESS TOFU: TAKE THE TOFU OUT OF THE PACKAGE(S). LINE A CONTAINER BIG ENOUGH TO HOLD THE BLOCK(S) OF TOFU WITH SEVERAL THICKNESSES OF PAPER TOWELS. PLACE THE TOFU ON TOP AND ADD ANOTHER LAYER OF SEVERAL THICKNESSES OF PAPER TOWELS. BALANCE A HEAVY WEIGHT (LIKE A PAN WITH SOME CANNED GOODS IN IT) ON TOP.

Bodacious
BAKED BANANA FRENCH TOAST

When you're craving a bigger, bolder breakfast, make this bodacious banana French toast. Prep this French toast the night before so she can have at least 8 hours of beauty rest before baking. Look for vegan brioche, or use stale sourdough or sandwich bread for a low-waste option.

SERVES 6

Coconut oil, for the baking dish

6 slices vegan brioche or thick stale bread

1 ripe banana

½ cup plain unsweetened soy milk or other nondairy milk

½ cup full-fat coconut milk

1 teaspoon pure vanilla extract

2 tablespoons spelt flour or all-purpose flour

1 tablespoon arrowroot powder or cornstarch

½ teaspoon ground cinnamon, plus more for sprinkling

⅛ teaspoon sea salt

¼ cup vegan chocolate chips, plus more for serving (optional)

Bananas, strawberries, oranges, and other fresh fruit, for serving

Vegan whipped cream, for serving

Pure maple syrup, for serving

Fresh mint, for garnish (optional)

1. Grease a 9 × 13-inch baking dish or Dutch oven with coconut oil. Halve the brioche slices and lay them evenly on the bottom of the dish.

2. In a medium bowl, mash the banana, then stir in the soy milk, coconut milk, and vanilla. Add the flour, arrowroot powder, cinnamon, and salt. Pour the mixture over the bread and let it sit in the refrigerator overnight (or at least 2 hours).

3. Preheat the oven to 350°F

4. Remove the bread from the fridge and allow the dish to come to room temperature as the oven warms.

5. Bake the French toast until the top has dried and is golden, about 30 minutes.

6. Meanwhile, in a microwave-safe bowl, microwave the chocolate chips in 20-second increments, stirring after each, until melted.

7. Drizzle the melted chocolate over the French toast. Serve with fresh fruit, vegan whipped cream, and maple syrup. Garnish with mint and chocolate chips, if desired.

Better BUTTERMILK WAFFLES

When you grow up in Georgia, you eat a whole lot of Waffle House. And then you go vegan, and you start to crave those perfect buttery waffles. So you figure out how to make them vegan at home. I've been making these exact vegan buttermilk waffles for a decade, and they never disappoint. The trick is to make your own vegan buttermilk by mixing plain unsweetened soy milk with vinegar. Let it sit and curdle for at least 5 minutes. The waffles can be made in any type of waffle iron, though American-style waffle irons are best. Get ready for the fluffiest, tastiest homemade waffles!

SERVES 6

1½ cups plain unsweetened soy milk

1 tablespoon apple cider vinegar or distilled white vinegar

1 tablespoon ground flaxseed meal

1½ cups all-purpose flour

⅓ cup cane sugar

½ teaspoon sea salt

1 teaspoon baking powder

½ teaspoon baking soda

2 teaspoons pure vanilla extract

6 tablespoons vegan stick butter, melted, plus more for the waffle iron

Pure maple syrup, for serving

Toasted pecans, for serving

Fresh fruit, for serving

1. Preheat the waffle iron according to the manufacturer's instructions.

2. In a small bowl, combine the soy milk and vinegar and let it sit for a few minutes while you work on the other ingredients. In another small bowl, mix the flaxseed meal and 2 tablespoons water and also let that sit to create a flax "egg."

3. In a large bowl, whisk together the flour, sugar, salt, baking powder, and baking soda. In another bowl, combine the soy milk mixture, flax egg, vanilla, and melted butter. Whisk to blend. Stir the milk mixture into the flour mixture until just combined.

4. Brush some vegan butter onto the waffle iron. Ladle about ½ cup of the batter into the waffle iron. Cook until golden brown, then transfer the waffle to a baking sheet and keep warm in the oven, or stack the waffles on a plate. Repeat with the remaining batter.

5. Serve the waffles with maple syrup, toasted pecans, and fruit.

NOTE: For a healthier option, swap out 4 tablespoons of the vegan butter for 4 tablespoons applesauce. And use ¼ cup sugar rather than ⅓ cup. These are so sweet, you don't need much syrup.

Wild Morning MUSHROOM AVOCADO TOAST

Ask yourself, could I live without avocado toast? If the answer is no, then prepare to unlock another level of devotion with this wild mushroom avocado toast. Inspired by one of my favorite restaurants in Los Angeles, Highly Likely, this nourishing breakfast packs tons of flavor and great texture. For the most delicious toast, use a mix of, or just one of, the following mushrooms: oyster, maitake, shiitake, king oyster, or chanterelle. And always start with great sourdough bread and a perfectly ripe avocado.

SERVES 2

2 tablespoons extra-virgin olive oil

2 garlic cloves, minced

½ pound assorted mushrooms, tough stems removed, chopped (if using king oyster mushrooms, try shredding them)

Sea salt

1 avocado, halved and pitted

2 slices sourdough bread

1 teaspoon sesame seeds

1 teaspoon nori flakes or dulse seaweed flakes

½ teaspoon grated orange zest

2 tablespoons minced fresh herbs, such as dill, cilantro, mint, and/or parsley

Freshly ground black pepper

1. In a skillet, heat the oil over medium-high heat. Add the garlic and sauté until slightly golden, about 30 seconds. Take care not to let it burn.

2. Reduce the heat to medium, add the mushrooms, and stir. Sprinkle in a pinch of sea salt and once the mushrooms begin to release their liquid, place a heavy pan on top of them. You could also use a bacon press, a lid, or a plate. Reduce the heat to medium-low and cook until tender and reduced in size, 5 to 8 minutes. Take a peek at the mushrooms halfway through to make sure they aren't burning. Sticking a little is okay and normal.

3. Stir the mushrooms to unstick them from the pan and season to taste with more salt.

4. Scoop the avocado into a bowl and mash it. Toast the bread and top with the mashed avocado. Season the avocado with a little salt, if desired, then top with the mushrooms.

5. Season with the sesame seeds, seaweed flakes, orange zest, fresh herbs, and black pepper.

Rose Tahini GRANOLA

Roses are for much more than Valentine's Day! Rose shines brightest when it's the focal point of a recipe—surrounded by more subtle, albeit equally divine, flavors and ingredients—and this rose tahini granola does just that.

One of the unique things about this recipe is that there is no added oil. Instead, we use tahini (sesame seed paste). Tahini dries as it bakes and makes this granola extra crunchy and delicious. It also adds protein, fiber, and lots of calcium to this morning delight.

SERVES 4

½ cup tahini

⅓ cup pure maple syrup

1 teaspoon pure vanilla extract

½ teaspoon ground cinnamon

¼ teaspoon sea salt

2 cups old-fashioned rolled oats

½ cup pistachios or other nuts or seeds

½ cup dried rose petals

1. Preheat the oven to 350°F. Line a baking sheet with parchment paper.

2. In a large bowl, combine the tahini, maple syrup, vanilla, cinnamon, and sea salt. Stir well. Stir in the oats and pistachios. Spread evenly onto the baking sheet in a thin layer. It will be very sticky.

3. Bake for 10 minutes.

4. Remove from the oven to flip and stir. Bake for another 5 minutes.

5. Allow the granola to cool for about 20 minutes (good luck, but it is worth the wait). Once cool, toss the granola with the dried rose petals and serve.

Savory Oats
BREAKFAST BOWLS

My daughter, Jorji, loves sweet steel-cut oatmeal for breakfast, but I prefer a savory breakfast. This savory oats breakfast bowl is the perfect compromise. I make steel-cut oats in the Instant Pot (which cooks them in a fraction of the time compared to the stovetop), season hers with maple syrup and cinnamon, and use the rest to make this tasty savory bowl. That's what you call "cutting two carrots with one knife." :)

SERVES 2

1 large sweet potato, peeled and cubed

1 pound oyster and shiitake mushrooms, thinly sliced or chopped

2 tablespoons extra-virgin olive oil

1 teaspoon sea salt

1 cup steel-cut oats

3 cups vegetable broth or 1 tablespoon Better Than Bouillon vegetable base stirred into 3 cups water

2 garlic cloves, minced (optional)

6 cups loosely packed spinach

TAHINI MISO SAUCE

1 tablespoon mellow (white) miso

1 tablespoon pure maple syrup

¼ cup tahini

2 tablespoons rice vinegar

ASSEMBLY

2 tablespoons toasted sesame seeds

Nori flakes or other seaweed flakes

1. Preheat the oven to 375°F.

2. In two separate bowls, toss the sweet potatoes and mushrooms with 1 tablespoon oil each and spread evenly on a baking sheet, keeping the sweet potatoes and mushrooms in their own areas. Sprinkle most of the salt onto the sweet potatoes and use what is left for the mushrooms.

3. Place the baking sheet with the sweet potatoes and mushrooms in the preheated oven. Roast the mushrooms until tender and slightly golden, 25 to 30 minutes. Slide the mushrooms off the baking sheet into a bowl.

4. Roast the sweet potatoes until tender, another 10 to 15 minutes. Do this in the evening, or during your meal-prep day, for greater ease in the morning.

5. Add the oats and 2 cups water to the Instant Pot. Stir. Seal and pressure cook on high for 7 minutes. Let the pressure release naturally.

6. Meanwhile, in a saucepan, bring the vegetable broth to a simmer. Add the garlic (if using) and spinach and cook until wilted but still bright green, about 30 seconds.

7. **MAKE THE TAHINI MISO SAUCE:** In a small bowl or a jar with a lid, combine the miso, maple syrup, tahini, and rice vinegar. Whisk and add water 1 tablespoon at a time to thin if necessary. If you are using a jar with a lid, tighten the lid on the jar and shake. You may need to use a fork to blend the miso. Add water to thin the sauce.

8. **ASSEMBLE THE BOWLS:** Add a scoop of the steel-cut oats to the bowls, then add the spinach/broth and roasted veggies. Top with the tahini miso sauce, sesame seeds, and seaweed flakes.

Addictive
SHIITAKE BACON

Becoming vegan doesn't mean you'll be forced to miss out on the joys of bacon. Mushrooms are so full of deep, umami flavor, and there's really no end to how they can transform in shape and texture once they hit the skillet. Just about any mushroom will work for this vegan bacon, but shiitakes are preferred for their meaty texture and rich flavor. While you can certainly enjoy this bacon for breakfast, it's a terrific addition to Miso Creamy Corn Pasta (page 153) and Perfect Pea Pesto Pasta (page 185). I also love adding shiitake bacon to salads and using it to top off a hearty bowl of Garlicky Greens & Grits (page 70). You can store this one in the fridge for 7 days but be warned: It rarely sticks around that long!

SERVES 2 TO 4

2 tablespoons soy sauce

1 tablespoon extra-virgin olive oil

2 teaspoons pure maple syrup

1 teaspoon liquid smoke

1 teaspoon smoked paprika

½ pound shiitake mushrooms, thinly sliced

1. In a small bowl, stir together the soy sauce, oil, maple syrup, liquid smoke, and smoked paprika.

2. Place the thin slices of mushrooms directly into the marinade and use your hands to gently massage. Let sit for at least 30 minutes.

3. Meanwhile, preheat the oven to 375°F. Line a baking sheet with parchment paper.

4. Lay the shiitake slices onto the parchment paper evenly, making sure not to overload the pan. They should have at least ⅓ inch of space between them.

5. Bake until dried out and crispy around the edges, about 20 minutes. Cook longer or shorter to your liking and then serve.

AIR-FRYER SHIITAKE BACON:

To make these in the air fryer, lay the marinated mushroom slices evenly in the air-fryer basket. Be careful to leave space around the mushrooms, and avoid layering. Air-fry at 350°F for 10 to 15 minutes, until your desired texture is achieved.

Beta-Boost
CARROT & MANGO MUFFINS

This is one of the earliest recipes from my blog, Sweet Potato Soul. In the original blog post I lament how silly it seems to buy a whole carton of eggs just to use one or two to make muffins, especially when you can use flaxseed meal instead. I was onto something.

This carrot and mango muffin recipe has been updated and upgraded since then, but every time I eat one I think back to those early days of my vegan journey. In my years as a vegan baker, I've learned that almond flour is the key to moist, fluffy muffins and quick breads. Almond flour also boosts the nutritional value of these muffins, which are also loaded with beta-carotene from the carrot and mango.

MAKES 12 MUFFINS

2 tablespoons ground flaxseed meal

1½ cups spelt flour

½ cup almond flour

½ cup packed light brown sugar

2 teaspoons baking soda

1 teaspoon ground cinnamon

½ teaspoon sea salt

½ cup plain unsweetened soy milk or other nondairy milk

1 tablespoon apple cider vinegar or distilled white vinegar

½ cup melted coconut oil or avocado oil

1 teaspoon pure vanilla extract

1 cup finely shredded carrots

¾ cup finely diced mango

½ cup raisins

½ cup chopped walnuts or pecans

1. In a small bowl, stir together the flaxseed meal and ¼ cup water. Let it sit for 5 minutes while you prepare the rest of the ingredients.

2. Preheat the oven to 350°F. Line 12 cups of a muffin tin with paper liners.

3. In a large bowl, combine the spelt flour, almond flour, brown sugar, baking soda, cinnamon, and salt. Stir well.

4. In another large bowl, combine the soy milk, vinegar, coconut oil, vanilla, carrots, mango, and raisins. Add the flaxseed mixture and stir well.

5. Pour the milk mixture into the flour mixture and stir to combine. Fold in the chopped walnuts.

6. Spoon the muffin batter into the lined muffin tin, filling each cup to the top.

7. Bake until the tops of the muffins are golden and pass the toothpick test, about 35 minutes. Leave them in the pan to cool before serving.

MAKE YOUR OWN ALMOND FLOUR BY BLENDING WHOLE ALMONDS. ONCE YOU HAVE A FINE FLOUR IT'S READY TO USE IN BAKING. MAKING YOUR OWN ALMOND FLOUR SAVES MONEY, AS STORE-BOUGHT ALMOND FLOUR IS USUALLY MORE EXPENSIVE THAN RAW ALMONDS.

Wholesome BUCKWHEAT CREPES

Buckwheat crepes are a nutrient-dense, gluten-free version of classic crepes. Buckwheat is high in protein, fiber, complex carbohydrates, iron, and zinc. Because these crepes are so thin, they reheat really well in the microwave, and are great for meal prep. I love to dress buckwheat crepes with Tantalizing Tahini Chocolate Sauce, but they're also delicious with savory fillings—think sautéed mushrooms and greens.

SERVES 6

1¼ cups buckwheat flour

½ cup rice flour

1 tablespoon arrowroot powder

1 cup plain unsweetened soy milk or other nondairy milk

1 teaspoon pure vanilla extract

1 tablespoon cane sugar

1 tablespoon ground flaxseed meal

Vegan stick butter or coconut oil, for the pan

FOR SERVING

Tantalizing Tahini Chocolate Sauce (page 241)

Fresh fruit

Toasted nuts

Pure maple syrup

Powdered sugar (optional)

1. In a blender, combine the buckwheat flour, rice flour, arrowroot, milk, 1½ cups water, the vanilla, sugar, and flaxseed meal.

2. Preheat a cast-iron skillet or other nonstick pan over medium heat. Grease the pan with butter.

3. Pour ½ cup of the batter into the center of the hot skillet. Carefully lift the pan and rotate to encourage the batter to spread out in a very thin round layer. If using a cast-iron skillet, you may need to use two hands—one in an oven mitt—to do this. Make sure you stand well away from the fire if using two hands. Cook until the batter is completely dry and cooked through, about 4 minutes, then flip. Cook the other side for about 2 minutes. Place the crepe in the middle of a folded dry kitchen towel and cover. Repeat with the remaining batter.

4. Serve the crepes with chocolate sauce, sliced fruit, toasted nuts, and maple syrup. Garnish with powdered sugar, if desired.

Garlicky GREENS & GRITS

This one is for all of my garlic, greens, and grits lovers! I love how versatile grits can be. From sweet to savory toppings, grits—cornmeal porridge—is the perfect creamy backdrop. I love starting my day with nutritious dark leafy greens. Greens are a rich source of fiber, vitamin K, potassium, and folate, plus many of the phytonutrients found throughout the fruit and vegetable world, like beta-carotene, lutein, and zeaxanthin. Starting your morning with greens is one of the healthiest ways to start the day.

SERVES 4

- 4 cups plain unsweetened soy milk or other nondairy milk
- 1 teaspoon sea salt, plus more to taste
- 3 tablespoons extra-virgin olive oil
- 1 cup white or yellow grits
- 1 teaspoon freshly ground black pepper
- 3 garlic cloves, minced
- 1 large bunch Swiss chard or beet greens, both leaves and stems thinly sliced, but kept separate
- ½ tablespoon soy sauce, plus more to taste
- 1 tablespoon fresh lemon juice

1. In a medium saucepan, bring the soy milk and ½ teaspoon of the salt to a simmer over medium heat. Add 1 tablespoon of the olive oil, the grits, and the black pepper and use a whisk to stir. Reduce the heat to low and continue to stir every few minutes until the grits are creamy and tender, 45 minutes to 1 hour.

2. Meanwhile, in a skillet, heat the remaining 2 tablespoons olive oil over medium heat. Add the garlic and the sliced chard stems. Sauté until the stems are tender and the garlic is fragrant and slightly golden, about 5 minutes.

3. Stir in the greens and ½ teaspoon salt, then add ½ cup water. Sauté until the greens are tender but still green, about 10 minutes. Add the soy sauce and lemon juice. Season to taste with more salt or soy sauce.

4. Serve the sautéed garlicky greens over the creamy grits.

DON'T THROW AWAY THE GREENS WHEN YOU BUY BEETS. THEY ARE TENDER, SAVORY, DELICIOUS, AND PERFECT FOR THIS RECIPE. LIKE CHARD AND SPINACH, BEET GREENS ARE A GREAT SOURCE OF BETA-CAROTENE, IRON, AND EVEN PROTEIN. FOR THIS RECIPE YOU CAN USE EITHER BEET GREENS OR CHARD, OR A COMBINATION. BE SURE TO USE THE CRUNCHY STEMS AS WELL. SIMPLY ADD THEM TO THE SKILLET TO SOFTEN BEFORE ADDING THE LEAVES. ENJOY WITH ADDICTIVE SHIITAKE BACON (PAGE 66) FOR A SMOKY ADDITION.

FUN & FANCY APPS & SNACKS

Leave the processed stuff on the shelves and make your own apps and snacks. It's healthier and cheaper, and they'll even taste better. Plus, if you have kids, it's a great way to get them involved in the cooking process. Baby J loves breaking up the tofu for Eat Mor Tofu Nuggets (page 102), helping me mix the sauce for Hot Stuff Harissa Almonds (page 92), and massaging the kale when we make Hot Cocoa Kale Chips (page 83).

Having friends over? Make a vegan platter with creamy Sunflower Cheese (page 84), Beet Lime Chutney (page 87), and Brilliant Beet Black Bean Dip (page 88). Many of the recipes in this chapter directly complement many of the mains in the entrée section of this cookbook. For example, the Red Roasted Potatoes (page 98) and Pop's Stellar Spinach (page 103) pair perfectly with the Tofu Salmon (page 160). For a Korean-inspired spin, try the Killer Kimchi Sweet Potato Pancake (page 76) and Gochujang Corn Ribs (page 79) in this section with the Korean Pulled 'Shroom Sandwiches (page 166).

Killer Kimchi

SWEET POTATO PANCAKE

My daughter, Jorji, goes absolutely wild for this recipe, and with good reason. Sweet potatoes are, of course, a favorite in our house, but when pan-fried together with tangy, sour kimchi, it's a whole new world of flavor. Savory pancakes are a staple of Korean cuisine, and sweet potatoes are a staple ingredient in both Korean and Southern cooking. I love how this recipe combines two very tasty cuisines.

SERVES 2 TO 4

- 1 cup matchsticks peeled sweet potato (about ½ sweet potato)
- 1 cup vegan kimchi, drained and chopped
- 4 scallions, white parts quartered lengthwise, dark green tops thinly sliced, for garnish
- ¾ cup all-purpose flour
- ¾ teaspoon sea salt
- 2 tablespoons toasted sesame oil or avocado oil

SLICING POTATOES CAN BE TIME-CONSUMING: TO SAVE TIME, USE YOUR FOOD PROCESSOR'S LARGE SHREDDER ATTACHMENT TO MATCHSTICK THE SWEET POTATO. TRADITIONAL KIMCHI, KOREAN FERMENTED VEGETABLES, IS NOT ALWAYS VEGAN (MANY ARE MADE WITH SEAFOOD PASTES), SO DOUBLE-CHECK THE LABEL TO BE SURE THAT YOU'RE PURCHASING A VEGAN VERSION.

1. In a bowl, combine the sweet potato matchsticks, chopped kimchi, and scallion whites.

2. In another bowl, combine the flour, ¾ cup water, and the salt and mix gently. Pour the flour mixture into the vegetables and stir well to combine.

3. Preheat a nonstick skillet over medium heat.

4. Add the oil to the hot skillet and pour the batter into the center. Use a spatula to spread the batter over the skillet and make a thin pancake. Reduce the heat to medium-low and cover the skillet. Cook for 15 minutes.

5. Uncover the skillet and use a spatula to loosen the pancake from the skillet. Remove from the heat, place the lid back on the skillet, and carefully flip the skillet, letting the pancake fall onto the lid. Return the skillet to the stove, turn the heat back to low, and use your spatula to help slide the intact pancake back into the skillet, cooked-side up.

6. Cook until the pancake is golden and the potatoes are tender throughout, 10 to 15 minutes.

7. Transfer the cooked pancake to a large plate or serving platter and let it cool for 5 minutes before slicing and serving. Garnish with the scallion greens.

Gochujang CORN RIBS

I've got just one problem with these ribs: They are gobbled up too darn fast! My gochujang corn ribs are the ultimate crowd-pleaser, and a recipe that's nearly as fun to make as it is to devour with loved ones. To capture that sweet, sticky taste of ribs, I let my corn marinate in the sauce for about 10 minutes to get extra saucy before cooking. These ribs are quick and easy to make, and I usually serve them when I have hungry guests. Everyone loves them!

SERVES 2 TO 4

- **4 ears corn, shucked**
- **¼ cup vegan gochujang (Korean chile paste)**
- **¼ cup soy sauce**
- **4 teaspoons toasted sesame oil**
- **4 teaspoons agave syrup**
- **4 teaspoons sesame seeds**
- **4 teaspoons fresh lime juice**
- **Lime wedges, for garnish (optional)**

I ADMIT IT'S NOT EASY TO SLICE THROUGH A CORN COB. ALWAYS USE A SHARP KNIFE, AS DULL KNIVES REQUIRE MORE EFFORT AND ARE PRONE TO SLIPPING AND ACCIDENTS. I'VE INCLUDED DIRECTIONS FOR HOW TO CUT AN EAR OF CORN INTO RIBS. BUT IF THAT IS STILL TOO HARD, TRY BOILING THE CORN FOR 10 TO 15 MINUTES AND ALLOWING IT TO COOL BEFORE CUTTING IT INTO RIBS.

1. Begin by cutting off the stem of 1 ear of corn. While the ear is lying on its side, cut it in half crosswise. Stand the now shorter piece of corn on its cut flat base and cut vertically down the center of the core. Lay the 2 pieces flat on the cutting board and cut each lengthwise in half to make a total of 4 thin pieces. Repeat with the other half and the remaining ears, for a total of 32 ribs (8 ribs per ear).

2. Preheat the oven to 375°F. Line a baking sheet with parchment paper.

3. In a small bowl, combine the gochujang, soy sauce, sesame oil, agave, sesame seeds, and lime juice. Stir well to combine.

4. Place the corn in a large bowl and coat with the sauce. Use your hands to toss the corn, and generously coat every part of it in the sauce. Let the corn and sauce sit for 10 minutes.

5. Arrange the corn ribs on the baking sheet and bake until the kernels are blistered and tender, about 25 minutes, flipping the corn ribs halfway through.

6. Serve hot out of the oven with lime wedges, if using.

AIR-FRYER CORN RIBS:

Place as many of the corn ribs as you can fit into the air-fryer basket. Air-fry at 375°F for 10 to 13 minutes, until the corn is tender and richly fragrant.

Beet
LATKES

Because my daughter, Jorji, is culturally mixed, I wanted to include this delicious recipe for beet and sweet potato latkes. If she could have it her way, Jorji would eat these on each of the eight nights of Hanukkah, when latkes are traditionally enjoyed in the Jewish faith. I love that these latkes are crispy on the outside, yet tender and delightfully chewy on the inside. And I especially love that they get Jorji to eat her beets.

SERVES 6

1 medium beet

1 small russet potato

1 small sweet potato

¼ yellow onion

1 tablespoon potato starch

2 tablespoons all-purpose flour

1½ teaspoons sea salt

Avocado oil, for shallow-frying

Applesauce, for serving

Vegan sour cream, for serving (optional)

Fresh herbs, for serving (optional)

JUST LIKE TRADITIONAL LATKES, YOU WANT TO MAKE SURE TO REMOVE AS MUCH LIQUID AS POSSIBLE FROM THE VEGETABLES BEFORE FRYING TO ENSURE MAXIMUM CRISPINESS. AFTER SHREDDING THE VEGGIES, USE PAPER TOWELS TO HELP SQUEEZE OUT ANY EXCESS LIQUID. FORM THE LATKE BATTER INTO TIGHT, ALMOST FLAT PATTIES BETWEEN THE PALMS OF YOUR HANDS BEFORE COOKING. THE EDGES SHOULD BE THINNER THAN THE CENTER, AND THE LATKES SHOULD HOLD TOGETHER BEFORE FRYING.

1. Preheat the oven to 225°F.

2. Line a large bowl with paper towels. Peel and grate the beet, both potatoes, and the onion into the bowl.

3. In another large bowl, combine the potato starch, flour, and salt.

4. Carefully use the paper towels to wring out excess liquid from the veggies, then transfer them to the bowl with the flour mixture. You may need to use multiple paper towels to get most of the liquid out of the veggies.

5. Toss the grated veggies with the flour mixture until well combined.

6. Line a large plate with three layers of paper towels and have near the stove. Pour ¼ inch of oil into a skillet or large pot and heat to about 350°F.

7. Form the batter into tight 3-inch latke patties and add as a many as will fit in the pan in a single layer. Fry until crispy and golden, 5 to 6 minutes per side. Transfer to the paper towels to absorb extra oil, then arrange on a baking sheet and keep them warm in the oven while you repeat with the rest of the batter, adding more oil if needed.

8. Serve with applesauce and vegan sour cream (if using).

AIR-FRYER BEET LATKES:

Grease the bottom of an air-fryer basket and fill the basket with latke patties. Grease the top of the latkes with spray oil or brush the tops with avocado oil. Air-fry at 350°F for 10 to 15 minutes. Flip and grease the other side of the latkes before cooking for another 8 to 10 minutes, or until golden and the veggies are tender.

Hot Cocoa
KALE CHIPS

When I first became a vegan blogger I was always experimenting with unique and unexpected flavor combinations. These hot cocoa kale chips are one of the creations that I still love ten-plus years later. Kale chips are an amazing snack, because despite being incredibly healthy, they crisp up like potato chips without loads of fat. When I have a snack craving, I usually pine for something savory and sweet and chocolate at the same time. These kale chips check all of the boxes.

SERVES 8

1 cup sunflower seeds

6 Medjool dates, pitted

2 tablespoons unsweetened cocoa powder

¼ teaspoon cayenne pepper

¼ teaspoon Himalayan pink salt or finely ground sea salt

1 bunch kale, leaves torn off the stems and midribs (about 10 cups leaves)

1. In a small bowl, soak the sunflower seeds in water to cover for 2 hours.

2. Preheat the oven to 325°F. Line two baking sheets with parchment paper.

3. Drain the sunflower seeds and rinse with fresh water. Place them in a food processor or blender along with the dates and ⅓ cup water. Blend until smooth-ish, then add the cocoa, cayenne, and salt and blend again.

4. Place the kale in a large bowl. Scoop the cocoa/sunflower seed puree onto the kale, and massage thoroughly with your hands for a few minutes. You may need to do this in batches. Transfer the massaged kale to the baking sheets and spread evenly, trying not to overlap the kale too much.

5. Bake until the kale is dry and crispy, about 30 minutes.

6. Let the kale chips cool for a few minutes before serving.

7. Store leftovers in an airtight container for 1 day.

Sunflower CHEESE

If your need for cheese is keeping you from becoming vegan, give this spreadable sunflower cheese a try. It's an easy-to-make take on creamy aged cheese, and is perfect for cheese plates and healthy snacking. Serve with vegan crackers, bread, or veggies on a cheese plate.

Nutritional yeast gives it a cheesy flavor, and mellow (white) miso adds sharpness and a little funk. While real cheese is known to cause inflammation in the body, the main ingredient in this vegan cheese, sunflower seeds, is a powerful anti-inflammatory food. Like all seeds, sunflower seeds are nutrient-packed. They're an excellent source of vitamin E, vitamins B1 and B6, iron, and so much more.

SERVES 8

1¾ cups sunflower seeds

½ cup nutritional yeast

2 teaspoons fresh lemon juice

1½ teaspoons mellow (white) miso or chickpea miso

½ teaspoon Dijon mustard

½ teaspoon onion powder

½ teaspoon garlic powder

½ teaspoon smoked paprika

¼ teaspoon ground turmeric

¼ teaspoon sea salt

Avocado oil, for the mold and spoon

1. In a medium bowl, soak the sunflower seeds in water to cover for at least 6 hours or overnight. Drain.

2. In a food processor, combine the sunflower seeds, nutritional yeast, lemon juice, miso, mustard, spices, and salt and blend until creamy.

3. Set a lightly oiled 4-inch round bottomless cheese mold (or tall ring mold) on a plate lined with parchment paper. Spoon the sunflower cheese into the mold. Use the back of an oiled spoon to press the sunflower cheese firmly into the mold and flatten the top. Then carefully remove the mold. (Alternatively, if you do not have a mold, shape it with your hands. Scoop the cheese out of the food processor onto a plate lined with parchment paper—try to form it into a mound. Then cover the cheese with plastic wrap and use your hands on the outside of the wrap to form it into a tight mound.)

4. Refrigerate for 1 hour to firm before serving.

Easy Peasy
CRISPY BEANS

Beans are great, but crispy beans are better! Despite the lengthy list of spices, these are super easy to make. Toss drained and rinsed beans in oil and then coat with the spices. Toss again, bake (or air-fry), and voilà: the perfect crispy snack or topping for salads and soups. You can use any bean for this recipe; just avoid red lentils or overcooked, mushy beans. I tend to use chickpeas, black beans, and even green lentils! Each bean has its own individual flavor and texture.

SERVES 4

2 (15-ounce) cans beans, drained and rinsed

1 tablespoon extra-virgin olive oil

1 teaspoon nutritional yeast

1 teaspoon dried oregano

1 teaspoon garlic powder

1 teaspoon cumin seeds

1 teaspoon smoked paprika

½ teaspoon sea salt

½ teaspoon freshly ground black pepper

1. Preheat the oven to 425°F. Line a baking sheet with parchment paper.

2. Place the beans in a bowl or directly onto the baking sheet. Drizzle the oil over the beans and toss. Sprinkle all the seasonings over the beans and toss well to coat.

3. Spread them evenly over the baking sheet and roast until crispy, about 20 minutes, before serving.

AIR-FRYER CRISPY BEANS:

Place the beans in a bowl and toss with the oil. Add the seasonings and toss well to coat. Transfer to the air fryer and cook at 400°F for 10 to 13 minutes, or until crispy.

Beet Lime
CHUTNEY

Beet lime chutney is a terrific and beautiful pairing for a cheese board. It's also delicious served over Black-Eyed Pea Curry (page 169) and Parsnip Carrot Curry (page 182). Make it when you meal-prep to have a nutritious and flavor-packed condiment you can add to sandwiches, eat as a snack, and mix into salads.

If you couldn't tell by the ample beet recipes in this cookbook, I LOVE BEETS! I love their earthy sweet taste, versatility, delicate texture, and health benefits. The main phytonutrients that give beets their characteristic deep red color are a powerful group of antioxidants called betalains. Beets are also a great source of folate, manganese, copper, and potassium—even better than bananas.

MAKES ABOUT 1½ CUPS

1 tablespoon coconut oil or extra-virgin olive oil

½ red onion, diced

4 small beets, steamed (see Note), peeled, and minced

3 tablespoons fresh lime juice

2 teaspoons raw cane sugar or coconut sugar

1 teaspoon grated fresh ginger

¼ teaspoon ground cumin

¼ teaspoon mustard seeds

1 teaspoon red chili flakes (optional)

1. In a medium saucepan, heat the oil over medium heat. Add the onion and cook until translucent, about 3 minutes. Add the beets, lime juice, and ½ cup water, and stir. Cook until the water begins to evaporate and the mixture thickens, about 7 minutes.

2. Stir in the sugar, ginger, cumin, mustard seeds, and chili flakes (if using). Cook for 5 minutes, stirring to make sure it does not burn. Remove from the heat and set aside to cool before serving.

NOTE ON STEAMED BEETS: Remove the stems of the beets and scrub well. Set a steamer insert or basket in a pot with several inches of water (or if using a steamer with short legs, you may need to use less water). Add the whole beets, cover, and bring water to a boil. Reduce to a simmer and cook until fork-tender, 40 to 45 minutes. (Larger beets may need to be cooked longer.) Check halfway through to make sure there is plenty of water left in the pot. Let the beets cool in the steamer basket, then peel them by placing under cold running water and rubbing the skin off with your fingers.

Brilliant Beet
BLACK BEAN DIP

In terms of taste, you cannot beat this dip. The flavor is savory and rich, with a subtle balance of sweetness from the beets. I always use miso in my hummus and bean dips because it adds a deeper umami edge.

For optimal health we should all eat beans every day. Why not hit your bean and beet consumption target by enjoying this glorious dip for a snack?

SERVES 4

1 (15-ounce) can black beans, drained and rinsed

1 red beet, steamed (see Note, page 87), peeled, and diced (½ to ¾ cup)

¼ cup chopped fresh parsley or other fresh herbs (cilantro, dill, mint, basil, etc.), plus a fresh herb sprig for garnish

1 garlic clove, chopped

1 teaspoon finely diced jalapeño pepper (optional)

1 tablespoon balsamic vinegar

1 tablespoon mellow (white) miso

1 teaspoon ground cumin

½ teaspoon freshly ground black pepper

2 tablespoons extra-virgin olive oil

Sea salt

1. In a food processor, combine the beans, beet, parsley, garlic, jalapeño (if using), balsamic vinegar, miso, cumin, and black pepper and blend until smooth. With the machine running, stream in the olive oil. Scrape down the side of the processor and blend some more. Season to taste with salt.

2. Serve at room temperature or chilled, garnished with the herb sprig.

Magical Mushroom HUMMUS

This chickpea dip is silky smooth and savory, topped with meaty sautéed mushrooms, and I use a little porcini mushroom powder to enhance the mushroom flavor. The trick to making luxuriously silky hummus is to use warm chickpeas. Freshly cooked and right out of the pot is best, but if you must use canned chickpeas, warm them in their liquid before blending. Make sure the beans are warm throughout.

MAKES 4 CUPS

MUSHROOM TOPPING

2 tablespoons extra-virgin olive oil

2 garlic cloves, minced

½ teaspoon cumin seeds

2 cups chopped mixed mushrooms: oyster, trumpet, maitake, Baby Bella

Sea salt

HUMMUS

3 cups cooked chickpeas, still warm, or 2 (15-ounce) cans, warmed (liquid reserved, see Note)

3 tablespoons tahini

1 tablespoon fresh lemon juice, plus more to taste

1 teaspoon ground cumin

1 teaspoon porcini mushroom powder or ½ teaspoon truffle mushroom powder

2 teaspoons mellow (white) miso

3 tablespoons extra-virgin olive oil, plus more for drizzling

About ¼ cup aquafaba, warmed (see Note)

Sea salt

Fresh parsley, for garnish

Freshly ground black pepper, for garnish

1. **MAKE THE MUSHROOM TOPPING:** In a skillet, heat the olive oil over medium heat. Add the garlic and cumin seeds and sauté until the garlic is fragrant and slightly golden, about 1 minute. Add the mushrooms and a pinch of salt and sauté over medium-low heat until the mushrooms are tender, about 15 minutes. As the mushrooms cook, place a heavy flat pot lid or bacon press directly on the mushrooms. This will help them become meatier, crispier, and more flavorful.

2. **MAKE THE HUMMUS:** While the mushrooms cook, combine the chickpeas, tahini, lemon juice, ground cumin, mushroom powder, and miso and blend until creamy in a food processor. With the machine running, slowly pour in the olive oil and then add aquafaba to thin. Add as much or as little as you would like to achieve your desired texture. I usually add around ¼ cup.

3. Season the hummus to taste with salt and lemon juice. Transfer the creamy hummus to a serving bowl. Top with the cooked mushrooms. Garnish with a generous drizzle of olive oil, fresh parsley, and black pepper.

NOTE: Aquafaba is the cooking liquid from home-cooked chickpeas or the liquid in the can for canned. When draining the home-cooked or canned chickpeas, be sure to save the aquafaba.

Hot Stuff Harissa ALMONDS

When it comes to the perfect snack, I like something crunchy, kinda sweet, and definitely salty. These harissa almonds check all of the boxes, and they're nutritious, too! Harissa is a red pepper sauce from North Africa. Like most pepper sauces, it's available in different spice levels, from mild to very spicy. Use whichever you like best in this recipe.

Feel free to swap out almonds for other nuts, sunflower or pumpkin seeds, or a mix of nuts.

SERVES 8

3 tablespoons harissa paste

3 tablespoons pure maple syrup

2½ cups raw almonds

1 teaspoon flaky sea salt, preferably Maldon

1. Preheat the oven to 350°F. Line a baking sheet with parchment paper.

2. In a medium bowl, stir together the harissa and maple syrup. Add the almonds and stir well to coat.

3. Spread the almonds over the baking sheet in an even layer. Sprinkle the sea salt over the nuts.

4. Roast for 10 minutes, then remove to stir the nuts. Continue roasting until fragrant and deeply browned, about another 10 minutes. Remove from the oven to cool and harden before serving.

Curry Crunch
PEPITAS

One of the easiest ways to elevate the flavor and texture in a basic salad, plain bowl of rice, or simple soup is to top it with these crunchy seasoned pepitas, also known as pumpkin seeds. They are an excellent source of vitamin K and zinc, each helpful for healing wounds and fighting against bacteria and viruses. These roasted seeds will be hot out of the oven, so be sure to let them cool before adding them to salads and soups, or enjoying them Jorji-style: one handful at a time.

MAKES 2 CUPS

2 cups raw pumpkin seeds

1 tablespoon melted coconut oil or avocado oil

1 teaspoon sea salt

1 teaspoon curry powder

1. Preheat the oven to 350°F. Line a baking sheet with parchment paper.

2. In a bowl, combine the pumpkin seeds and coconut oil and stir thoroughly. Add the salt and curry powder and stir again. Spread the pumpkin seeds over the baking sheet in an even layer.

3. Roast until fragrant and golden brown, about 8 minutes.

4. Allow them to cool completely before eating and serving.

Crispy Cranberry
BRUSSELS SPROUTS

This savory/sweet Brussels sprouts recipe is inspired by my favorite appetizer at Bar Margot, a restaurant in the Four Seasons Hotel in Atlanta. Hot and crispy-on-the-outside Brussels sprouts are tossed in a sticky maple-lemon sauce for the ultimate healthy comfort food. In the original version from Bar Margot, the Brussels sprouts are deep-fried, but I prefer to roast them for this at-home version. They are so easy to make, and absolutely addictive.

SERVES 4

1 pound Brussels sprouts

1½ tablespoons extra-virgin olive oil

2 tablespoons fresh lemon juice, plus more to taste

1 tablespoon pure maple syrup

1 teaspoon garlic powder

½ teaspoon sea salt

¼ cup dried cranberries

1. Preheat the oven to 375°F.

2. Trim the bottoms off of the Brussels sprouts and halve them lengthwise. Large Brussels can be quartered. Place the sliced veggies in a bowl.

3. In a small bowl, combine the oil, lemon juice, maple syrup, garlic powder, and salt. Whisk to blend, then pour half of the sauce over the Brussels and toss well.

4. Transfer the Brussels to a baking sheet or cast-iron skillet (hold on to the bowl). Roast until the outer leaves are crispy and golden and the veggies are tender, 15 to 20 minutes.

5. Transfer the Brussels back to the bowl and toss with the remaining sauce and the dried cranberries. Serve hot.

Sticky Fingers EDAMAME

Most of us have tried steamed edamame tossed with sea salt at a Japanese restaurant—yum! That's how I enjoy my edamame for a healthy snack many days of the week. But have you ever had edamame tossed in a spicy sesame ginger sauce? It's healthy snacking on a whole 'nother level! To temper the heat in this recipe, omit the chili-garlic paste.

Rich in protein, fiber, vitamin K, folate, and soy-specific antioxidants, edamame can be found in the frozen vegetable section of most large grocery stores. Make sure to buy edamame (green soybeans still in the pod) and not the shelled version, which may be labeled mukimame. Sucking edamame out of the pod makes them ten times more enjoyable.

SERVES 2 TO 4

Kosher salt

1 pound frozen edamame in the pod

2 tablespoons toasted sesame oil

2 garlic cloves, minced

1 tablespoon minced fresh ginger

1½ teaspoons cane sugar

1 tablespoon tamari or regular soy sauce

1 tablespoon chili-garlic paste

1 teaspoon sesame seeds, for garnish

1. Bring a pot of salted water to a boil. Add the edamame and cook for 5 minutes. Drain and set aside.

2. In a skillet, heat the sesame oil over medium heat. Add the garlic and ginger and sauté until the garlic is fragrant and slightly golden, about 1 minute.

3. In a small bowl, stir together the sugar, 2 tablespoons water, the tamari, and chili-garlic paste. Pour the mixture into the skillet and stir as it comes to a simmer. Remove the skillet from the heat.

4. Add the edamame and toss it in the sauce to coat.

5. Garnish with the sesame seeds and serve immediately.

Red Roasted POTATOES

As much as I adore sweet potatoes, I also love good ol' white potatoes. Actually, I love every variety of potato: purple, yellow, white, and red. And they all can stand in for the red-skinned potatoes in this recipe—even sweet potatoes. The spices used on these roasted potatoes are my absolute favorite for everyday veggie roasting. I use it on roasted cauliflower and broccoli, even beans. Keep these spices stocked in your kitchen for whenever a roasted veggie craving strikes.

SERVES 4

1 pound red potatoes, quartered

1 tablespoon extra-virgin olive oil or avocado oil

2 teaspoons nutritional yeast

1 teaspoon sea salt

½ teaspoon dried oregano

½ teaspoon garlic powder

½ teaspoon smoked paprika

Chopped fresh parsley, for garnish

1. Preheat the oven to 375°F. Line a large baking sheet with parchment paper.

2. In a bowl, toss the potatoes with the olive oil, nutritional yeast, salt, oregano, garlic powder, and smoked paprika. Spread evenly on the baking sheet.

3. Roast until the potatoes are tender, fragrant, and crispy on the edges, 40 to 45 minutes. Garnish with parsley before serving.

Orange Cauliflower BITES

Is it a snack, an appetizer, or an entrée? That's all up to you. Like its main ingredient, cauliflower, this tasty dish is Ms. Versatile. I give instructions for making these crispy cauliflower bites in the oven or air fryer. Use whichever is more convenient for you. Air-frying does produce a crispier cauliflower in half the time of the oven, but I like that oven baking results in a more tender, juicy cauliflower center.

Serve these cauliflower bites as an appetizer, or make them the main meal by serving over brown rice. Garnish with shaved red cabbage, cilantro, sesame seeds, or your favorite toppings. The dish also pairs well with the Korean Pulled 'Shroom Sandwiches (page 166) and the Mushroom Bulgogi Lettuce Cups (page 176).

SERVES 4

CAULIFLOWER BITES

¾ cup all-purpose flour or gluten-free flour

1 teaspoon garlic powder

½ teaspoon sea salt

1 cup plain unsweetened soy milk or other nondairy milk

1 small head cauliflower, cut into bite-size pieces

Spray oil

ORANGE SAUCE

1 tablespoon coconut oil or avocado oil

2 tablespoons minced fresh ginger

3 garlic cloves, minced

1 cup freshly squeezed orange juice (2 to 3 oranges)

⅓ cup soy sauce

3 tablespoons rice vinegar

3 large Medjool dates, pitted

1½ tablespoons cornstarch

1. **MAKE THE CAULIFLOWER BITES:** In a bowl, combine the flour, garlic powder, salt, and soy milk. Stir well, then add the cauliflower pieces to the mixture and stir to thoroughly coat.

2. Preheat the oven to 375°F. Line a baking sheet with parchment paper.

3. Remove the cauliflower from the batter and shake off any excess before placing the cauliflower on the parchment paper in an even layer. Keep at least ½ inch of space between the pieces. Spray the tops of the cauliflower with oil.

4. Bake until crispy and golden, 30 to 35 minutes.

5. **MAKE THE ORANGE SAUCE:** In a saucepan, heat the oil over medium heat. Add the ginger and garlic and cook until fragrant and slightly golden, about 1 minute. Add the orange juice, soy sauce, rice vinegar, and dates. Bring to a simmer and cook for 5 minutes.

6. Meanwhile, in a small bowl, stir the cornstarch into ¼ cup water until dissolved.

7. Remove the sauce from the heat and stir in the cornstarch mixture. Stir until it begins to thicken, about 1 minute. Allow the sauce to cool for a bit, then transfer it to a blender and blend until smooth.

8. Add the crispy cauliflower to a large bowl and pour the sauce over. Toss to coat all of the cauliflower pieces and serve immediately.

AIR-FRYER CAULIFLOWER BITES:

Make the batter and toss the cauliflower bites in it as directed. Grease the bottom of the air-fryer basket with spray oil. Remove the cauliflower from the batter and shake off any excess before placing the cauliflower into the air fryer in an even layer. Keep at least ½ inch of space between the pieces. Spray the tops of the cauliflower with oil. Air-fry at 350°F for 15 to 20 minutes, or until crispy and golden. Make the sauce and continue as directed.

Eat Mor Tofu NUGGETS

Not sure about tofu? These tender nuggets will make you a fan. Growing up, I loved Chick-fil-A chicken nuggets. Though I haven't eaten chicken since 2008, I still remember those juicy tender chicken nuggets, and their savory crispy coating. My daughter doesn't feel deprived when she sees her friends munching on real nuggets, and all of her friends love these vegan nuggets, too!

SERVES 4

- 1 (14-ounce) block extra-firm tofu, pressed (see To Press Tofu, page 54) for 20 minutes
- 2 tablespoons dill pickle juice or caper juice
- 2 tablespoons tamari soy sauce
- ½ teaspoon cane sugar
- 2 tablespoons extra-virgin olive oil
- 1 tablespoon all-purpose flour
- 1 teaspoon garlic powder
- ½ teaspoon smoked paprika
- ½ teaspoon freshly ground black pepper
- ½ to 1 teaspoon sea salt, to taste
- Spray oil
- Ketchup or vegan BBQ sauce, for serving

1. Use your hands to break the pressed tofu into nugget-size pieces, dropping them into a large bowl. These can be as large or small as you'd like, but keep in mind that they will reduce in size as they cook.

2. In a separate bowl, mix the dill pickle juice, tamari, sugar, and oil. Pour the mixture over the tofu and toss well. Sprinkle the all-purpose flour, garlic powder, smoked paprika, pepper, and salt over the tofu and stir to coat.

3. Spray oil on the bottom of the air-fryer basket. Pour the tofu into the basket and spread evenly. Spray more oil onto the tops of the tofu nuggets.

4. Cook in the air fryer at 375°F for 20 minutes, flipping halfway through. If the tofu is still not crispy after 20 minutes, cook for another 5 minutes. Be careful not to burn.

5. Serve with ketchup.

OVEN-BAKED TOFU NUGGETS:

Preheat the oven to 375°F. Line a baking sheet with parchment paper. Spread the nuggets out on the baking sheet evenly and coat with spray oil. Bake until golden brown and crispy on the edges, about 40 minutes, flipping halfway through.

NOTE: Reheat vegan chicken nuggets in an air fryer or toaster oven. In the air fryer, 5 minutes at 350°F should do the trick. In the oven, warm the nuggets at 350°F for 10 minutes.

These vegan chicken nuggets can be frozen for up to 3 months. Don't thaw before reheating, just reheat from frozen, either in the air fryer or the oven, following the original cooking instructions.

Pop's
STELLAR SPINACH

I get my creativity in the kitchen from my dad. He's always coming up with interesting yet simple ways to bring new life to everyday ingredients. The first time I had this sautéed spinach with sun-dried tomatoes, I couldn't believe I hadn't always been making spinach like this. It's so simple, but it's bursting with flavor from the savory blend of garlic, sun-dried tomatoes, and soy sauce. Enjoy this stellar spinach as a side to the Tofu Salmon (page 160).

SERVES 4

2 tablespoons extra-virgin olive oil

3 garlic cloves, minced

10 ounces fresh spinach

Sea salt

¼ cup oil-packed or dry-packed sun-dried tomatoes, chopped

1 tablespoon tamari soy sauce, plus more to taste

1. In a skillet, warm the olive oil over medium-high heat. Reduce the heat to medium, add the garlic, and cook until fragrant and slightly golden, about 1 minute.

2. Cook the spinach in batches. Add the first batch to the skillet along with a pinch of salt and cook, stirring, until wilted, about 2 minutes. Continue adding the spinach and salt until all the spinach is wilted.

3. Add the sun-dried tomatoes and tamari and cook until the spinach is tender, about 8 minutes. Season to taste with more tamari before serving.

Bali Shaved BRUSSELS

This Brussels sprouts recipe is inspired by a meal I made in Bali with wild foraged fiddlehead fern shoots, hand-grated coconut, lime juice, and fried shallots—a Balinese staple. That was in 2011, but the culinary memories I have from that trip still linger. Brussels sprouts are an unlikely replacement for tender baby fiddlehead ferns, but they do an exceptional job of carrying the rich Southeast Asian–inspired ingredients.

SERVES 2 TO 4

½ cup unsweetened shredded coconut

1 tablespoon coconut oil

2 shallots, thinly sliced

4 cups very thinly sliced Brussels sprouts

2 sweet peppers, seeded and thinly sliced, or ½ red bell pepper, thinly sliced

1 teaspoon red chili flakes

2 tablespoons pure maple syrup

2 tablespoons soy sauce, plus more to taste

Lime wedges, for squeezing

1. Preheat the oven to 350°F.

2. Spread the shredded coconut on a baking sheet and toast for 5 minutes.

3. In a large wok or skillet, melt the coconut oil over medium-high heat. Add the sliced shallots and cook until translucent, about 3 minutes. Add the Brussels sprouts and peppers and cook over medium heat until they're tender, about 10 minutes.

4. Remove from the heat. Add the chili flakes, maple syrup, and soy sauce. Stir well and season with more soy sauce to taste. Serve with a squeeze of lime juice and a generous sprinkling of toasted coconut on top.

Jerk Sweet Potato
STREET FRIES

When I have a choice between traditional fries and sweet potato fries, the sweet potatoes always win. I love any combination of savory and sweet, and these jerk fries are what sweet potato fry dreams are made of. They're messy, colorful, bursting with flavor, and they're easy to make. Not to mention, they're doused in wonderful Jamaican jerk seasoning powder and a sensational mix of scallions, nutmeg, black pepper, and thyme.

Serve them hot, right out of the air fryer or oven. Speaking of air fryers, I like using this gadget for the crispiest sweet potato fries, because it takes a shorter amount of time to get the yummy crunch.

SERVES 2 TO 4

2 sweet potatoes, peeled and sliced like fries, as thick or thin as you'd like

3 tablespoons avocado oil or extra-virgin olive oil

2 teaspoons jerk seasoning (salt-free, if desired)

1 teaspoon garlic powder

1 teaspoon sea salt

1 teaspoon dried thyme

½ red bell pepper, diced

4 scallions, diced, white and green parts kept separate

1 garlic clove, minced

1 tablespoon minced or grated fresh ginger

½ teaspoon black peppercorns

½ teaspoon freshly grated nutmeg

1 teaspoon grated lime zest, for garnish

Chopped fresh cilantro, for garnish

Lime wedges, for squeezing

1. Preheat the air fryer to 375°F.

2. In a bowl, toss the sweet potato fries with 1 tablespoon of the oil, the jerk seasoning, garlic powder, salt, and thyme.

3. Spread the sweet potato fries evenly into the basket of the air fryer. Air-fry for 10 to 15 minutes, or until crispy and browned on the edges.

4. Meanwhile, in a saucepan, warm the remaining 2 tablespoons oil over medium heat. Add the bell pepper, scallion whites, garlic, ginger, whole peppercorns, and nutmeg and sauté for 1 minute. Remove from the heat.

5. When the sweet potatoes are out of the air fryer, transfer them to a serving platter and spoon the sautéed peppers and spices over them.

6. Garnish with the lime zest, cilantro, scallion greens, and a generous squeeze of lime juice. Serve immediately.

OVEN-BAKED JERK SWEET POTATO FRIES:

Spread the coated fries on a baking sheet lined with parchment paper. Bake in a 375°F oven until crispy and browned on the edges, about 35 minutes. Make the sautéed peppers as directed. When the fries come out of the oven, plate and garnish as above.

SUPER-SATISFYING SALADS & SOUPS

The recipes in this chapter are inspired by Atlanta's diverse culinary traditions and my experiences of eating all around the globe. My Collard Greens Miso Soup (page 137) is a warm, fragrant, and wholesome meeting between Japan and the American South, enlivened by garlic, red chili flakes, and, of course, miso. My Watermelon Gazpacho (page 134)—a recipe I created with my family, as an homage to my time living in Spain—allows me, for a few spoonfuls, to go back in time to a truly wonderful and transformative period of my life.

The key to making fantastic soups and salads is understanding seasoning and flavor balance. Acidity is essential to a good salad, and the best have an element of sweetness to level out the acidic notes. You can elevate your own salads by playing with natural sweeteners like pure maple syrup, pomegranate molasses, or one of my favorite natural sweeteners, agave. Fresh herbs will enhance any dish. And don't forget the salt to pull it all together. If you weren't one already, the recipes in this chapter will turn you into a salad and soup lover.

Fennel Beet SALAD

My dad is so picky about everything! Everything except this beet salad, that is. In this beautiful pink-and-green salad, fennel and beets pair up to deliver bite after bite of crunchy, citrusy goodness.

If you're new to fennel, it tastes and smells a bit like licorice, and contrasts really well with beets. Similar to the texture of celery, you get a bit of crunch in every bite of the salad. And because fennel doesn't get soggy, and beets take on more flavor as they marinate, this salad is perfect for meal prep.

SERVES 4

1 large fennel bulb

4 beets, steamed (see Note, page 87), peeled, and cut into ½-inch cubes

¼ red onion, thinly sliced

Lemon Vinaigrette (page 247)

Sea salt

Toasted pumpkin seeds (see Note, page 113), for garnish

1. Cut the stalks and fronds off the top of the fennel bulb. Save a few of the fronds for garnish; save the rest for stock or compost. Thinly slice the entire fennel bulb. Use a mandoline to do this, if you have one. If not, slice as thinly as you possibly can using a sharp knife.

2. In a large bowl, combine the beets, fennel, and onion. Add the vinaigrette and use your hands to toss. Season to taste with salt.

3. Garnish with the fennel fronds and pumpkin seeds.

Kimchi Kale SALAD

Not all salads need dressing! So how do you transform kale into a tender and tasty treat? Kimchi and avocado. All kale needs to go from tough to tasty is fat, salt, and acid. Massage the kale with avocado, lemon juice, and salt to tenderize the leaves, then add kimchi to finish off the flavor. The perfect salad has just the right amount of sweetness to it, in this case roasted sweet potatoes. You may be surprised when this becomes your new favorite entrée salad. Make it even more filling by adding cooked quinoa or farro.

SERVES 2

- 1 sweet potato, peeled and cut into ½-inch cubes
- 1 tablespoon extra-virgin olive oil or avocado oil
- ¾ teaspoon sea salt, plus more to taste
- 5 cups thin strips kale (about 1 large bunch), stems and midribs removed
- 1 avocado, cubed
- 2 tablespoons fresh lemon juice
- ½ cup vegan kimchi
- 1 cup Easy Peasy Crispy Beans (page 85), made with chickpeas, or plain cooked chickpeas
- 3 tablespoons toasted pumpkin seeds (see Note)
- 1 teaspoon fennel seeds

CUT THE KALE INTO THIN STRIPS FOR THE MOST TENDER TEXTURE. NOT ONLY WILL THE KALE'S TEXTURE BE BETTER, ITS NUTRIENTS WILL BECOME MORE BIOAVAILABLE TO YOU AS YOU CONSUME IT.

1. Preheat the oven to 375°F. Line a baking sheet with parchment paper.

2. In a bowl, toss the sweet potatoes with the oil and ½ teaspoon of the salt. Spread them evenly on the baking sheet and bake until tender, about 35 minutes.

3. Place the kale in a large bowl. Add half the avocado, the lemon juice, and ¼ teaspoon sea salt. Using your hands, massage the avocado into the kale until the greens are tender, about 2 minutes.

4. Add the other half of the avocado, the kimchi, chickpeas, sweet potatoes, pumpkin seeds, and fennel seeds and toss well. Season to taste with salt.

NOTE: Spread the pumpkin seeds in a small baking pan and toast in a 350°F oven until fragrant and slightly golden, about 8 minutes.

Naked Niçoise SALAD

Make no mistake, this vegan Niçoise salad is stripped of eggs and tuna, but it is fully dressed in top-notch flavor and texture. To veganize, chickpeas stand in for eggs, and artichoke hearts for tuna. The roasted veggies, salty capers, and quality olive oil make this vegan version shine so bright. Finish it off with homemade Niçoise dressing. There are a lot of beautiful salads in this cookbook, but this might be the prettiest.

SERVES 4

½ pound little red or multicolored potatoes, halved

1½ tablespoons extra-virgin olive oil or avocado oil

½ teaspoon dried oregano

½ teaspoon garlic powder

½ teaspoon sea salt, plus more to taste

½ teaspoon freshly ground black pepper

1 bunch asparagus, woody ends trimmed

8 romaine lettuce leaves

8 radicchio leaves (or use more romaine if you can't find radicchio)

1½ cups cherry tomatoes, halved

1 cup jarred marinated artichoke hearts

1 (15-ounce) can chickpeas, drained and rinsed

¼ cup jarred green or black olives, pitted and halved

2 tablespoons capers

Niçoise Dressing (page 246)

Sprigs of parsley, mint, basil, and/or fennel, for garnish

1. Preheat the oven to 375°F.

2. In a bowl, toss the potatoes with 1 tablespoon of the oil, then sprinkle on the oregano, garlic powder, salt, and pepper. Spread evenly in a 9 × 13-inch baking dish and roast until tender, 30 to 35 minutes.

3. Toss the asparagus in the remaining ½ tablespoon oil, spread on a baking sheet, and roast at the same time as the potatoes, until fork-tender, about 20 minutes. (Alternatively, toss the asparagus in the oil and grill in an indoor grill pan or on an outdoor grill.)

4. Place the romaine and radicchio leaves onto plates. Top with the roasted potatoes, asparagus, tomatoes, artichoke hearts, chickpeas, olives, and capers.

5. Drizzle the dressing over the salads. Garnish with fresh herbs.

Peach
WHITE BEAN SALAD

Summer in a salad! This peach and white bean salad was made for summer cookouts and packed cooler lunches by the beach. Allow the veggies and beans to marinate in the peach miso dressing before serving for next-level flavor. Every ingredient is nutritious, so you can feel confident that you're giving your body what it needs when you go for thirds of this salad.

SERVES 8

7 cups cooked white beans or 4 to 5 (15-ounce) cans, drained and rinsed

3 ears corn, grilled and kernels cut from the cobs, or 2 cups fire-roasted frozen corn, thawed

4 heirloom tomatoes, diced

1 peach, diced

3 radishes, thinly sliced

¼ medium red onion, thinly sliced

½ jalapeño pepper, seeded and minced (optional)

About 1 cup chopped mixed fresh herbs, such as basil, dill, mint, cilantro, and/ or parsley, plus more for garnish

Peach Miso Dressing (page 245)

Sea salt and freshly ground black pepper

1. In a large bowl or serving bowl, combine the beans, corn, tomatoes, peach, radishes, onion, jalapeño (if using), and about 1 cup of the herbs.

2. Pour the dressing over the salad and toss well. Season to taste with salt and black pepper. Garnish the salad with any remaining herbs and serve.

Lovely
LENTIL
SWEET
POTATO
SALAD

I make a big lentil salad every week of the year. This salad can be enjoyed on its own, tossed with lettuce, enjoyed on toast, or served with a whole grain. And as with bean salads, it gets tastier as it marinates, making it perfect for meal prep.

Go crazy with the fresh herbs here. I can't say this enough: You can never have too many fresh herbs! I love spreading this potato salad on avocado toast in the morning, or tossing it into my lettuce or kale salad in the afternoon. For best results, allow the lentils to cool completely before making the salad, and use a firm variety of lentils such as French Puy, black, or green lentils. Whatever you do, be sure not to overcook the lentils. Enjoy this flavorful salad at room temperature or chilled.

SERVES 4

- 2 small sweet potatoes, peeled and cut into ½-inch cubes
- 1 tablespoon extra-virgin olive oil
- 1 teaspoon garlic powder
- 1 teaspoon smoked paprika
- 1½ teaspoons sea salt
- 1 cup dried French Puy lentils, sorted and rinsed, or 2 cups cooked lentils
- ¼ red onion, diced (about ¼ cup)
- ⅓ cup each fresh basil, dill, cilantro, and mint, chopped
- Pomegranate Vinaigrette (page 249)
- Toasted pumpkin seeds (see Note, page 113), for garnish
- Lime wedges, for squeezing
- Pomegranate seeds, for garnish (optional)

1. Preheat the oven to 375°F. Line a baking sheet with parchment paper.

2. In a bowl, toss the cubed sweet potato with the oil, garlic powder, smoked paprika, and 1 teaspoon of the salt. Spread evenly onto the baking sheet and roast until tender, 30 to 40 minutes.

3. In a saucepan, combine the uncooked lentils, ½ teaspoon salt, and 2 cups water and bring to a simmer. Cook over medium heat until tender, about 30 minutes. Let them cool completely.

4. In a large bowl, combine the roasted sweet potatoes, lentils, red onion, and fresh herbs. Drizzle the pomegranate vinaigrette over the salad and toss to coat. Serve garnished with toasted pumpkin seeds, lime wedges, and pomegranate seeds (if using).

Dilly Broccoli SALAD

I've talked a lot about the protein you get from beans, chickpeas, and lentils, but you can find plenty of protein in vegetables, too. Broccoli in particular is packed with protein, as well as fiber, vitamins C and K, and lots of other good stuff that helps with heart and immune health. This salad makes it super simple to access all of that goodness in less than 20 minutes. To honor the nutritional value of this recipe, steam the broccoli for no more than 5 to 7 minutes. Steamed broccoli should be bright green.

SERVES 4

1 head broccoli, florets and stalk chopped (about 3 cups)

3 Persian (mini) cucumbers, diced (about 2 cups)

¼ red onion, thinly sliced

¼ cup chopped fresh dill

¼ cup chopped fresh parsley and mint

Miso Tahini Sauce (page 236)

1 teaspoon sea salt, plus more to taste

½ teaspoon freshly ground black pepper

½ teaspoon cayenne pepper, or more to taste

¼ cup almonds, chopped toasted or raw

Grated lemon zest, for garnish

1. Fill a large bowl with ice and water and have at hand. Set up a steamer: a basket, insert, or rack and a pot for the water. Add 1 to 2 inches of water to the pot (but not enough to touch the basket). Cover and bring the water to a boil. Add the broccoli, cover tightly, and steam until crisp-tender and bright green, 5 to 7 minutes; you don't want to overcook it. Transfer the broccoli from the steamer to the ice bath. Let it sit for about 5 minutes.

2. Use a slotted spoon to transfer the broccoli to a bowl. Add the cucumbers, red onion, dill, parsley and mint, miso tahini sauce, and salt and toss well. Season with the black pepper, cayenne, and more salt to taste.

3. Sprinkle the almonds and lemon zest on top of the salad.

Rad Strawberry SALAD

As gorgeous as it is tasty, this summer salad is so rad. Radicchio, part of the chicory family, is a leafy Italian vegetable with a bold, bitter taste. I'm a big fan of bitter radicchio, but I'll admit, despite being balanced here with mild romaine, starchy chickpeas, and sweet strawberry vinaigrette, it is not everyone's cup of tea. If you aren't a fan, replace the radicchio with shredded red cabbage or more romaine.

SERVES 2 TO 4

1 head romaine lettuce, chopped

½ to 1 head radicchio, chopped

⅓ cup Strawberry Vinaigrette (page 247)

½ recipe Easy Peasy Crispy Beans (page 85), made with chickpeas

¼ shallot, thinly sliced

Sliced strawberries, for garnish

In a large salad bowl, combine the chopped romaine and radicchio. Pour the vinaigrette over the salad and toss.

Serve the salad topped with the crispy chickpeas, shallot, and sliced strawberries.

Big & Bulky
CURRIED KALE SALAD

This hearty salad is my everyday entrée salad. I load this baby up with a range of produce, like oranges, sweet potatoes, and cauliflower. Kidney beans provide an excellent source of protein, and the cooked bulgur is both comforting and adds extra sustenance. Do take the time to make the curried pepitas, which add the best crunch to this big and bulky salad.

SERVES 4

1 small head cauliflower, chopped

2 tablespoons extra-virgin olive oil

1½ teaspoons sea salt

1 teaspoon garlic powder

1 sweet potato, peeled and cut into ½-inch cubes

5 cups chopped kale, stems and midribs removed

¼ to ½ cup Curry Vinaigrette (page 248), to taste

2 cups cooked red kidney beans or other beans, or Easy Peasy Crispy Beans (page 85), made with chickpeas

2 cups cooked bulgur or quinoa

2 large oranges, sectioned

½ cup Curry Crunch Pepitas (page 94)

1. Preheat the oven to 375°F. Line two baking sheets with parchment paper.

2. In a large bowl, toss the cauliflower with 1 tablespoon of the olive oil, 1 teaspoon of the salt, and ½ teaspoon of the garlic powder. Spread evenly on one of the baking sheets.

3. In the same bowl, toss the sweet potato with the remaining 1 tablespoon olive oil, ½ teaspoon salt, and ½ teaspoon garlic powder. Spread them evenly onto the second baking sheet.

4. Put the cauliflower and sweet potato in the oven and roast until both are tender, about 35 minutes for the cauliflower, and closer to 40 to 45 minutes for the sweet potatoes.

5. Place the chopped kale in the same bowl and drizzle with ¼ cup of the curry vinaigrette. Use your hands to massage the dressing into the kale until it has reduced in size by about half.

6. Add the cauliflower, sweet potato, beans, and bulgur. Toss well and season with more dressing to taste.

7. Top with the sectioned oranges and curried pepitas.

Silky Sweet Potato
BISQUE

Creamy, rich, and herbal, this is one of my favorite soups. To give it a luxuriously silky texture, I use naturally creamy white cannellini beans in place of cream. Not only do the beans successfully replace dairy, they add more protein and fiber. Cannellini beans are also a great source of calcium, iron, and potassium. Bisques shouldn't be all creaminess, though. Finish this one off with crispy rosemary white beans for a welcome crunch in every bite.

SERVES 4

3 tablespoons extra-virgin olive oil or avocado oil

2 garlic cloves, minced

½ yellow onion, diced

2 medium-large sweet potatoes, peeled and cut into ½-inch cubes

1½ cups cooked cannellini beans or 1 (15-ounce) can, drained and rinsed

1 tablespoon Better Than Bouillon vegetable base, 1 vegetable bouillon cube, or 3 cups vegetable broth

1 teaspoon freshly ground black pepper

½ teaspoon cayenne pepper

Crispy Rosemary White Beans (page 128; optional), for garnish

1. In a large heavy-bottomed pot, heat the oil over medium heat. Add the garlic and onion and sauté until the onion turns translucent, about 3 minutes.

2. Add the sweet potatoes and cannellini beans. If using bouillon base or cubes, mix with 3 cups water and add to the pot. If using broth, just add to the pot.

3. Bring to a boil. Reduce to a simmer and cook until the sweet potatoes are tender, about 20 minutes.

4. Remove from the heat and stir in the black pepper and cayenne. Use an immersion blender (see Note) to puree the soup until silky smooth.

5. Serve the bisque garnished with some of the crispy white beans, if desired.

NOTE: I recommend an immersion blender to puree this soup. If you plan on using a stand blender, allow the soup to cool to a safe temperature (cool enough to eat) before blending and be sure to open the steam vent in the lid.

CRISPY ROSEMARY WHITE BEANS

Similar to the Easy Peasy Crispy Beans (page 85), these white beans add a welcome crunch and burst of flavor to soups and salads. They also make a great healthy snack.

- 1 (15-ounce) can cannellini or navy beans, drained and rinsed
- 1 tablespoon extra-virgin olive oil
- 1 teaspoon minced fresh rosemary
- 1 teaspoon garlic powder
- 1 teaspoon smoked paprika
- ½ teaspoon sea salt
- ½ teaspoon freshly ground black pepper

1. Preheat the oven to 425°F. Line a baking sheet with parchment paper.

2. Place the beans in a bowl or directly onto the baking sheet. Drizzle the oil over the beans and toss. Sprinkle the rosemary, garlic powder, smoked paprika, salt, and pepper over the beans and toss well to coat.

3. Spread them evenly over the baking sheet and roast until crispy, about 20 minutes.

AIR-FRYER CRISPY ROSEMARY WHITE BEANS:

Preheat the air fryer to 375°F. Transfer the seasoned beans to the fryer basket and spread as evenly as possible, then fry for 15 minutes, or until crispy,

Party-Hearty KALE SOUP

Just like the name suggests, this soup is a party in a bowl. While this soup is of course great for lunch or dinner, I love eating it for breakfast! Hearty and filled with all sorts of good stuff—think cannellini beans, lentils, potatoes, fennel seeds, and oh so much more—this Italian soup tastes as good as it smells. It's incredibly hearty on its own, but you can also serve it with a fat slice of sourdough for a complete experience.

SERVES 8

- 3 tablespoons extra-virgin olive oil
- 1 large leek (well washed, white part only), sliced ¼ inch thick, or 1 yellow onion, diced
- 3 garlic cloves, minced
- 3 celery stalks, diced
- Sea salt
- 1 (28-ounce) can diced tomatoes
- 2 carrots, diced
- 2 cups ½-inch cubes peeled honeynut or butternut squash
- 2 cups ½-inch cubes fingerling or Yukon Gold potatoes
- 1 (15-ounce) can cannellini beans or 1½ cups freshly cooked
- 1 cup cooked lentils (any type, except for red lentils)
- 2 vegetable bouillon cubes, 2 tablespoons Better Than Bouillon vegetable base, or 6 to 8 cups vegetable broth

- 1 bay leaf
- 1 large sprig fresh rosemary
- 2 teaspoons dried basil
- 1 teaspoon dried thyme
- 1½ teaspoons fennel seeds
- 1 teaspoon red chili flakes, plus more for serving

- ½ bunch kale leaves (stems and midribs removed), chopped (about 4 cups)
- 1 teaspoon freshly ground black pepper
- 1 loaf sourdough or Italian bread, such as ciabatta, sliced and toasted, for serving

1. In a large heavy-bottomed pot, heat the olive oil over medium-high heat. Add the leek, garlic, celery, and a dash of salt and sauté until they begin to soften, about 5 minutes.

2. Pour in the diced tomatoes and stir well. Add the carrots, squash, potatoes, beans, and lentils. Stir well and let the vegetables simmer in the tomatoes for 2 minutes.

3. Add the bouillon cubes and 6 cups water (or 6 cups veggie broth), followed by the bay leaf, rosemary, basil, thyme, fennel seeds, and chili flakes. Stir well. If you'd like the soup more soupy, add up to 2 cups more water or broth.

4. Bring to a boil, then reduce to a light simmer, partially cover, and cook until the hard veggies (carrots and potatoes) are tender, about 30 minutes. Stir the kale into the soup in the last 5 minutes of cooking. Add the black pepper and season to taste with salt.

5. Though I don't usually remove the rosemary sprig or the bay leaf, be careful they don't end up in the serving bowl. Serve the soup with a thick slice of toasted bread and a sprinkle of red chili flakes.

Cozy CHICKPEA TOMATO SOUP

Years ago my stepmom, Tracy, made a deeply flavorful chickpea tomato soup for me when I was sick with a cold. As soon as I felt better I got to work on re-creating her masterpiece. Chickpeas, butternut squash, fire-roasted tomatoes, and warm aromatic spices combine to create a delicious lightly pureed soup. It's the perfect balance of savory, sweet, and acid. It feels like a warm hug during the coldest days of winter.

To raise the comfort food factor, serve this soup with vegan grilled cheese. I make mine with good-quality sourdough and vegan cheese from Violife or Daiya. Baby J won't eat soup, but I can get her to use this soup as a dip when vegan grilled cheese is involved!

SERVES 6

2 tablespoons extra-virgin olive oil

1 yellow onion, diced

3 garlic cloves, minced

1 tablespoon minced or grated fresh ginger

1½ teaspoons ground cumin

1 teaspoon ground coriander

1 teaspoon smoked paprika

½ teaspoon ground turmeric

¼ teaspoon ground cinnamon

4 cups diced peeled butternut squash

1 (28-ounce) can or 2 (14.5-ounce) cans fire-roasted diced tomatoes

3 cups cooked chickpeas or 2 (15-ounce) cans, drained and rinsed

2 teaspoons Better Than Bouillon vegetable base

1 teaspoon kosher salt, plus more to taste

1 teaspoon freshly ground black pepper

Fresh cilantro, for garnish

1. In a large pot, heat the olive oil over medium heat. Add the onion, garlic, and ginger and sauté until the onion is translucent, about 3 minutes. Sprinkle in the cumin, coriander, smoked paprika, turmeric, and cinnamon and stir. Toast the spices for 30 seconds.

2. Add the butternut squash, diced tomatoes, chickpeas, 3 cups water, bouillon base, and salt. Bring to a simmer and cook until the butternut squash is tender, about 30 minutes.

3. Use an immersion blender (see Note, page 126) to puree the soup. I prefer my soup to be slightly chunky.

4. Add the black pepper and season to taste with more salt. Garnish with cilantro.

Beet Sweet Potato
SOUP

Beets are the heart of this Southern take on borscht. This soup is naturally sweet thanks to the combination of beets, sweet potatoes, and carrots, and is punctuated with pungent ginger, spicy bits of jalapeño, and salty bouillon base. A few tablespoons of red wine vinegar adds a really nice layer of elegance, so I love to serve this at dinner parties.

SERVES 6

3 beets, with greens attached (see Note)

1 tablespoon grapeseed oil

½ yellow or red onion, diced

4 garlic cloves, minced

1 jalapeño pepper, seeded and minced

1½-inch knob fresh ginger, minced or grated (about 2 tablespoons)

1 celery stalk, chopped (about 1 cup)

1 carrot, diced (about 1 cup)

6 cups vegetable broth, or 1 tablespoon Better Than Bouillon vegetable base (plus more to taste, optional) or 1 bouillon cube dissolved in 6 cups water

½ teaspoon freshly ground black pepper, plus more to taste

1 sweet potato, peeled and cut into ½-inch cubes

2 small Yukon Gold or red potatoes, cubed

3 to 4 tablespoons red wine vinegar or apple cider vinegar

Sea salt

1 cup chopped fresh parsley, for garnish

1. Cut the tops off the beets. Chop enough of the stems to get ½ to 1 cup. Chop enough of the leaves to get 2 cups. Trim and peel the beets and cut them into ½-inch cubes (about 2 cups).

2. In a large Dutch oven or soup pot, heat the oil over medium heat. Add the onion, garlic, jalapeño, ginger, celery, and beet stems and sauté until the onions are translucent, about 5 minutes. Add the beets and carrots and sauté for 3 minutes.

3. Add the vegetable broth and black pepper. Add more broth or water to thin the soup, if you'd like. Bring it to a boil, then reduce to a simmer, partially cover, and cook for 10 minutes. Add the sweet potato and Yukon Gold potatoes and continue to cook until the veggies are tender, another 20 minutes.

4. Stir in the beet greens and cook until tender, about 5 minutes. Remove from the heat and stir in the red wine vinegar. Season to taste with salt and/or vegetable base. Serve hot garnished with the fresh parsley.

NOTE: If you can't get beets with greens, use Swiss chard leaves and stems to take the place of the beet stems and greens.

Minimalist Mushroom BISQUE

Mushrooms are the epitome of savory, more accurately described as umami. Make this minimalist mushroom bisque and taste the complexity and richness of these fabulous fungi. With just six ingredients, it is so incredibly easy to make. I recommend a blend of mushrooms, ideally a mix of oyster, maitake, and cremini (aka Baby Bella).

SERVES 4

2 tablespoons extra-virgin olive oil

½ yellow onion, diced

2 pounds assorted mushrooms, such as oyster, maitake, and cremini, chopped

1 teaspoon dried thyme

6 cups water mixed with 1½ tablespoons Better Than Bouillon vegetable base, or 6 cups vegetable broth

Sea salt and freshly ground black pepper

1. In a soup pot, heat the oil over medium-high heat. Add the onion and sauté over medium-high heat until translucent, about 5 minutes. Add the mushrooms and cook until tender, 5 to 8 minutes.

2. Add the thyme, water, and bouillon base. Bring to a simmer, cover, and cook for 1 hour.

3. With an immersion blender (see Note, page 126), puree the soup in the pot.

4. Season to taste with salt and black pepper.

Watermelon GAZPACHO

In college, I lived in Madrid for one semester. I still consider it one of the best experiences of my life. Nearly every day, my señora served some sort of chilled soup, most often Spanish gazpacho. This watermelon gazpacho is my Southern-girl spin on the classic chilled tomato soup. Sweetness from the watermelon is balanced by fresh herbs, vinegar, and savory tamari soy sauce. For a final touch, serve the soup topped with crispy toasted bread crumbs and flaky salt. Use summer's freshest ingredients for the tastiest soup. Shout-out to my dad, stepmom, and brother DeMion for helping me nail this recipe!

SERVES 6

4 cups cubed watermelon

2 large ripe tomatoes, chopped

1 large cucumber, peeled and chopped

1 sweet or yellow onion, chopped

1 garlic clove, peeled but whole

¼ cup fresh basil leaves

¼ cup fresh tarragon leaves

¼ cup fresh dill leaves and stems

¼ cup red wine vinegar, plus more to taste

1 tablespoon tamari soy sauce, plus more to taste

1 teaspoon sea salt

Fresh herbs, for garnish

Fresh bread crumbs, toasted in oil, for serving

Maldon flaky sea salt, for serving

Extra-virgin olive oil, for drizzling

1. In a blender, combine the watermelon, tomatoes, cucumber, onion, garlic, basil, tarragon, dill, vinegar, tamari, and salt and blend until your ideal gazpacho texture is achieved. I like mine thicker than a smoothie, not quite a smooth puree. Season to taste with more tamari and vinegar.

2. To serve, garnish with fresh herbs, toasted bread crumbs, flaky sea salt, and a drizzle of olive oil.

Collard Greens
MISO SOUP

My mom doesn't like to cook, but she will happily make this recipe. It's easy, nutritious, restorative, and delicious. This is like a traditional Japanese miso soup, but uses collard greens instead of seaweed—though nori is a welcome addition. Collard greens are rich in calcium, vitamin K, beta-carotene, and vitamin C. Collards are also rich in sulforaphane, a compound found in cruciferous vegetables that has anticancer benefits.

Miso is rich in probiotics, but those gut-healthy bacteria can be destroyed when heated to excess. To preserve the probiotics in the miso, dissolve it in a bowl of cooled broth from the soup, then stir the miso mixture back into the soup before serving.

SERVES 4

½ bunch collard greens (about ½ pound)

1 garlic clove, minced

1½ teaspoons grated fresh ginger

2 scallions, sliced, white and green parts kept separate

1 cup cubed firm tofu (about 7 ounces)

2 teaspoons red chili flakes

1 cup hot water

¼ cup mellow (white) miso or yellow miso, plus more to taste

1 teaspoon soy sauce, plus more to taste

1 teaspoon toasted sesame oil, plus more for serving

1. Cut out the midribs and stems of the collard leaves. Roll the leaves up lengthwise into a cigar shape and cut them crosswise into ½-inch-wide ribbons (4 to 5 cups).

2. In a large pot, bring 5 cups water to a boil. Add the garlic, ginger, and scallion whites. Reduce the heat to medium-low and simmer for 5 minutes.

3. Add the collard leaves, tofu, and chili flakes. Cover the pot and cook until the collards are tender, 5 to 8 minutes. Remove from the heat and allow the soup to cool until safe to eat.

4. In a bowl, stir 1 cup of the soup into the miso until it has dissolved. Add the miso liquid to the pot and stir well.

5. Season with the soy sauce and sesame oil. Add more miso and/or soy sauce to taste.

6. Serve warm, topped with a few sliced scallion greens and a couple drops of toasted sesame oil.

Seaside STEW

A vegan mash-up of cioppino stew and clam chowder, this stew gets its body from mushrooms. I use a variety of mushrooms for textural interest and loads of flavor, but the real trick to making this creamy stew taste like the sea is ume plum vinegar and nori seaweed. Ume vinegar has a briny flavor, so I use it in all of my sea-inspired recipes. Before I became vegan I could not imagine abstaining from seafood. Turns out what I loved so much about seafood is the same ocean essence found in seaweed. Nori is the type of seaweed used to wrap sushi—salty, tender, and tastes like the sea.

SERVES 4 TO 6

2 tablespoons extra-virgin olive oil or avocado oil

3 shallots, chopped

3 garlic cloves, minced

¼ pound oyster mushrooms, chopped

6 shiitake mushrooms, sliced

1 (5-ounce) package enoki mushrooms, tough bottoms removed

Kosher salt

5 canned hearts of palm, cut into ½-inch-thick chunks

5 medium red potatoes, quartered

1 cup full-fat coconut milk

1 tablespoon Better Than Bouillon vegetable base, plus more to taste

1 teaspoon dried thyme

2 tablespoons ume plum vinegar, plus more to taste

6 sheets nori, cut into strips

Fresh parsley and/or dill, for garnish

1. In a Dutch oven or large pot, warm the oil over medium-high heat. Add the shallots and garlic and sauté until the shallots are translucent, a few minutes.

2. Add all of the mushrooms and a pinch of salt. Cook until the mushrooms begin to release their liquid and soften, about 5 minutes.

3. Add the hearts of palm, potatoes, coconut milk, 2½ cups water, the bouillon base, and thyme. Stir well and cook until the potatoes are tender, 15 to 20 minutes.

4. Remove from the heat and stir in the ume plum vinegar and nori strips. Season to taste with more ume plum vinegar and salt or bouillon base.

5. Serve hot garnished with fresh parsley and/or dill.

EVERYDAY ENTRÉES

You'll love the satisfying and delicious entrées in this chapter. From meaty pasta to West African–style stew, I've got you covered. Unlike an animal-based entrée, you can eat these vegan dishes in abundance. Each entrée is made with wholesome ingredients and boasts protein, fiber, plus myriad nutrients found in plants. Some of the dishes are very easy to make, while others require a little more prep. To cut prep time in half I recommend using a food processor or a mechanical food chopper to dice and mince the veggies.

I think everyone should determine what an entrée means to them. So much of this is defined by one's culture, one's appetite, and one's own tastes and preferences in vegan cooking. Veggies, beans, and grains deserve more shine than they are used to getting on the dinner plate.

Righteous Rigatoni BOLOGNESE

This is one of Baby J's favorite meals, which warms my heart because it was my favorite meal when I was little, too. My nana is an amazing cook, but the meal I loved most growing up was her rigatoni Bolognese: fat, round noodles with a savory, sweet red gravy and ground turkey. When I gave up poultry in 2008, Nana quickly swapped out the turkey for vegan grounds, and it tasted the same! And when I became a vegan chef, I swapped out the store-bought vegan grounds for hearty lentils and walnuts. Believe it or not, the combination of cooked lentils and ground walnuts makes the best wholesome replacement for ground meat. Not only will this simple replacement save you money— we all know how expensive plant-based meat alternatives are—it has way less sodium, fat, and additives.

SERVES 4

2 tablespoons extra-virgin olive oil

4 garlic cloves, minced

1 cup walnuts, finely minced by hand or in a food processor

2 cups cooked green lentils

1 (15-ounce) can tomato sauce

2 tablespoons tomato paste

1 teaspoon dried basil

1 teaspoon dried thyme

1 teaspoon dried oregano

1 teaspoon cane sugar, plus more to taste

1 teaspoon sea salt, plus more to taste

1 teaspoon freshly ground black pepper

8 ounces rigatoni

Fresh basil or parsley, for garnish

1. In a skillet, warm the oil over medium heat. Add the garlic and sauté until fragrant and slightly golden, about 1 minute. Be careful not to burn it. Stir in the walnuts and toast until fragrant, about 3 minutes.

2. Add the lentils, tomato sauce, tomato paste, ¼ cup water, the dried herbs, sugar, salt, and pepper. Stir well and bring to a simmer. Cover and cook over medium-low heat for as long as it takes you to make the pasta.

3. In a pot of boiling water, cook the rigatoni according to the package directions (I usually cook mine for 12 minutes).

4. Taste the sauce and season with more sugar and salt if necessary.

5. Drain the pasta and toss with the sauce. Garnish with basil or parsley. Serve and enjoy!

Coconut Black Bean STEW

Growing up we ate beans every day. Like many Black kids of my generation, beans were a staple of my diet because they were nutritious, dirt cheap, and culturally significant. Still are! This stew is inspired by the black bean soup I loved as a kid. I think cumin was created for black beans, and this soup has one of the yummiest broths ever. I usually make it in the Instant Pot. Serve over brown rice and with veggies for a complete meal.

SERVES 4

1 tablespoon coconut oil or avocado oil

1 teaspoon ground coriander

1 teaspoon cumin seeds or ground cumin

½ red onion, diced

3 garlic cloves, minced

1 tablespoon minced fresh ginger

½ bell pepper, diced

1½ cups dried black beans, soaked overnight

1 large sweet potato, peeled and cubed (about 1½ cups)

2 cups vegetable broth or water

1 (13.5-ounce) can full-fat coconut milk

1 tablespoon Better Than Bouillon vegetable base or 1 bouillon cube (skip this if you're using veggie broth)

2 tablespoons fresh lime juice

Sea salt

Cayenne pepper

Perfect Every Time Brown Rice (page 237), for serving

Fresh cilantro, chopped, for garnish

1 jalapeño pepper, thinly sliced, for garnish

Lime wedges, for squeezing

1. In a large Dutch oven, heat the oil over medium heat. Add the ground coriander and cumin seeds and toast until fragrant, about 30 seconds. Add the onion, garlic, ginger, and bell pepper and sauté until the onion begins to soften, about 3 minutes.

2. Add the black beans, sweet potato, and vegetable broth. Bring to a boil, then reduce to a simmer, partially cover, and cook the beans until firm-tender, about 35 minutes.

3. Add the coconut milk (and bouillon, if you're not using vegetable broth). Stir well and cook until the stew has thickened and the beans are tender, about 15 minutes. Stir in the lime juice and season to taste with salt and cayenne.

4. Serve over rice and garnish with the fresh cilantro and jalapeño, plus a squeeze of lime juice.

INSTANT POT BLACK BEAN STEW:

1. Soak the beans overnight, if desired. Turn the Instant Pot on to Sauté and let heat for 10 minutes. Add the oil to the pot. Once warm, add the ground coriander and cumin seeds and toast for about 30 seconds. Add the onion, garlic, ginger, and bell pepper and sauté until the onion begins to soften, about 3 minutes. Cancel the Sauté setting.

2. Stir in the black beans and sweet potato. Add the coconut milk and only 1 cup veggie broth (or 1 cup water plus bouillon base). Seal the Instant Pot and pressure cook for 25 minutes for soaked beans, or 30 minutes for unsoaked beans. Allow the pressure to release naturally. Stir in the lime juice and season to taste with salt and cayenne. Serve over rice and garnish with the cilantro and jalapeño pepper, plus a squeeze of lime juice.

Moroccan-Spiced CAULIFLOWER

I was lucky enough to travel to Morocco during my time living in Spain. It was then that I fell in love with the cuisine of North Africa. This dish is ingredient-heavy, but you really want that array of spices to capture the essence of Moroccan flavors. To make this recipe process more seamless, measure out all of the spices in a single bowl before you start cooking (known in the cooking world as "mise en place"). The dried fruits, to me, really make this dish characteristic of North African cooking, as do the chickpeas, citrus, and deeply aromatic spice blend.

SERVES 4 TO 6

- 2½ tablespoons extra-virgin olive oil
- ½ yellow onion, diced
- 1 red bell pepper, diced
- 4 garlic cloves, minced
- 1 tablespoon minced fresh ginger
- 2½ teaspoons smoked paprika
- 1½ teaspoons ground cumin
- 1½ teaspoons ground coriander
- 1 teaspoon freshly ground black pepper, plus more to taste
- 1 teaspoon cumin seeds (optional)
- 1 teaspoon ground turmeric
- ½ teaspoon ground cinnamon
- 1 (14.5-ounce) can diced tomatoes
- 1 medium head cauliflower, chopped
- 1½ cups cooked chickpeas or 1 (15-ounce) can, drained and rinsed
- 2 tablespoons raisins
- 2 tablespoons chopped dried apricots or dates
- 2½ cups vegetable broth or 2 teaspoons Better Than Bouillon vegetable base stirred into 2½ cups water
- ¼ cup freshly squeezed orange juice (about 1 small orange)
- 1½ teaspoons sea salt, plus more to taste
- Fresh cilantro or parsley, for garnish
- Lemon wedges, for squeezing

1. In a large skillet or pot, heat 2 tablespoons of the olive oil over medium-high heat. Once warm, add the onions, bell pepper, garlic, and ginger and sauté until onions are translucent, about 3 minutes.

2. Add the smoked paprika, ground cumin, coriander, black pepper, cumin seeds (if using), turmeric, and cinnamon. Stir well and toast the spices until fragrant, about 30 seconds.

3. Add the tomatoes, cauliflower, chickpeas, raisins, apricots, vegetable broth, orange juice, and salt. Bring the stew to a simmer over medium heat and cook until the cauliflower is tender, 8 to 12 minutes. Season to taste with salt and pepper.

4. Serve garnished with fresh herbs and lemon wedges.

Green Jackfruit CHILI

Jackfruit has been an important ingredient in Southeast Asia and the Caribbean for centuries. Make sure you purchase green unripe "young" jackfruit for this recipe. Ripe jackfruit has an incredible sweet flavor reminiscent of Jolly Ranchers but is not suitable for savory dishes. The jackfruit shredding process does take a bit of time, but you'll want that shredded texture to really experience this dish.

The base of this chili isn't tomatoes, but tomatillos—the staple ingredient of salsa verde. Tomatillos look like green tomatoes but grow encased in a papery husk. I adore their acidic taste, and I add sugar to the chili to balance the tang.

SERVES 4

1½ pounds fresh tomatillos, husks removed, rinsed

2 poblano peppers

1 jalapeño pepper

3 garlic cloves, unpeeled

2½ tablespoons avocado oil

1 cup loosely packed fresh cilantro (about ½ bunch), plus more for garnish

1 yellow onion, diced

2 (20-ounce) cans young green jackfruit, drained and shredded with a fork

2 teaspoons dried oregano

1 teaspoon chili powder

1 teaspoon ground cumin

½ teaspoon garlic powder

½ teaspoon smoked paprika

1 teaspoon sea salt, plus more to taste

1½ cups cooked pinto beans or 1 (15-ounce) can, drained and rinsed

1½ tablespoons cane sugar

2 teaspoons Better Than Bouillon vegetable base

2 tablespoons soy sauce

Freshly ground black pepper

White rice or Perfect Every Time Brown Rice (page 237), for serving

1. Turn on the broiler.

2. Arrange the tomatillos, poblanos, jalapeño, and garlic in a broilerproof baking dish and toss with ½ tablespoon of the oil. Broil about 4 inches away from the heat until the peppers are tender and charred, about 20 minutes. Let the vegetables cool completely before removing the seeds and skins from the charred peppers. Take the garlic cloves out of their skins, too.

3. In a blender, combine the tomatillos, peppers, garlic, and cilantro and blend until smooth.

4. In a large pot, warm the remaining 2 tablespoons oil over medium heat. Add the onions and sauté until tender and translucent, about 3 minutes. Add the shredded jackfruit, oregano, chili powder, cumin, garlic powder, smoked paprika, and salt and sauté until the jackfruit begins to brown, about 5 minutes.

5. Add the beans, sugar, tomatillo puree, 1½ cups water, the bouillon base, and soy sauce and bring to a simmer. Cook until thick and fragrant, about 15 minutes.

6. Season to taste with salt and black pepper and serve hot with rice, garnished with fresh cilantro.

Roasted Grape BULGUR PILAF

I'm not really a grape girl, but I go crazy for roasted grapes. Roasting draws all the complexity to the surface of the grapes, and their juiciness transforms into succulence. Sure, roasting grapes may destroy most of their antioxidants, but I promise you, it is worth it. Instead of rice, bulgur is the foundation of this roasted grape pilaf. Bulgur has an earthy, nutty flavor, but offers much more fiber and protein than rice. Feel free to substitute freekeh, a Middle Eastern grain that shares a similar texture, but has a complex smoky taste. Look for both at your local international or Middle Eastern market, at Whole Foods, or online.

SERVES 6

½ pound seedless red grapes

1½ teaspoons extra-virgin olive oil

⅛ teaspoon sea salt, plus more to taste

1½ cups bulgur or freekeh (roasted cracked wheat)

3 cups water or vegetable broth

1¾ cups cooked chickpeas or 1 (15.5-ounce) can, drained and rinsed

2 cups chopped mixed fresh herbs, such as cilantro, parsley, mint, dill, and/or basil

1 cup Curry Vinaigrette (page 248; see Note)

¼ cup toasted slivered almonds or toasted pumpkin seeds (see Note, page 113)

1. Preheat the oven to 350°F.

2. In a baking dish large enough to hold the grapes in a single layer, toss the grapes with the olive oil and salt. Spread evenly and roast until the grapes are tender, about 30 minutes.

3. Meanwhile, in a medium pot, combine the bulgur and water and bring to a boil. Reduce the heat to a simmer, partially cover, and cook for 10 minutes. Remove from the heat, completely cover with the lid, and let sit for 5 to 10 minutes, or until ready to use.

4. In a large bowl, toss the cooked bulgur with the grapes, chickpeas, herbs, and curry vinaigrette. Season to taste with more salt.

5. Garnish with the toasted nuts just before serving.

NOTE: If you cooked the bulgur in a salted broth, reduce the amount of salt in the vinaigrette.

Miso Creamy Corn PASTA

No shade on American-style cream pastas, but they're a little extra. All that sauce, I feel like I'm eating soup with a fork. I'm bougie, so I like my creamy pastas how they do it in Italy, or at least in Rome, where I fell in love with al dente pasta dressed in a light but sensational cream sauce.

But how did we get from Rome to miso creamy corn pasta? I love pasta from Italy, I love Southern corn, and I love miso from Japan! This pasta combines all those culinary gems in a unique yet delicious pasta.

SERVES 4

2 tablespoons kosher salt

8 ounces linguine

3 tablespoons extra-virgin olive oil, plus more for drizzling

3 garlic cloves, minced

1 cup corn kernels, fresh or frozen

Sea salt

2 teaspoons mellow (white) miso

2 tablespoons nutritional yeast

½ teaspoon freshly ground black pepper, plus more to taste

1 teaspoon red chili flakes (optional)

Fresh parsley, for garnish

Walnut Parmesan (page 236)

1. Bring a pot of water to a boil for the pasta. Add the kosher salt and linguine and cook according to the package directions (I usually cook my linguine for 8 to 9 minutes). Reserving at least ½ cup of the pasta water, drain the pasta. Don't rinse, but toss with a drizzle of olive oil.

2. In a large skillet, heat the 3 tablespoons olive oil over medium heat. Add the garlic and corn, plus a dash of sea salt, and cook until the garlic is fragrant and slightly golden, about 3 minutes.

3. Dissolve the miso in ¼ cup of the hot pasta water, then pour it into the skillet with the garlic and corn. Sprinkle in the nutritional yeast and pepper and stir well. Bring the mixture to a simmer and continue to stir until it is creamy, about 2 minutes. Add more pasta water if you want a thinner sauce.

4. Add the pasta to the skillet and use tongs to toss and coat. Season to taste with salt and pepper. Serve with red chili flakes (if using), parsley, and walnut parmesan.

Black Bean Crust
PIZZA

Who knew black beans were so versatile? When cauliflower pizza crust became all the rage I was inspired to play around with other ingredients to make a more nutritious pizza crust. Black beans are the perfect choice. This recipe uses flax egg to hold the crust together, and as the black bean crust dehydrates in the oven it transforms into a light and fluffy pizza base. Sure, it's black, but I think that makes it more fun.

SERVES 4

PIZZA CRUST

3 tablespoons ground flaxseed meal

2 (15-ounce) cans black beans, drained and rinsed

3 tablespoons nutritional yeast

2 garlic cloves, minced

1 to 1½ teaspoons sea salt

½ teaspoon cayenne pepper

TOPPING

Extra-virgin olive oil

1 cup sliced shiitake mushrooms

1 red onion, thinly sliced

½ cup of your favorite pizza sauce

1 cup shredded vegan mozzarella cheese

3 cups chopped kale, spinach, or arugula

2 cups thinly sliced, peeled butternut squash, roasted (see Notes)

DID YOU KNOW THAT THE PIGMENTS IN BLACK BEANS THAT GIVE THEM THEIR DEEP BLACK COLOR ARE CALLED ANTHOCYANINS? THIS GROUP OF PHYTONUTRIENTS HAS POWERFUL ANTIOXIDANT AND ANTI-INFLAMMATORY BENEFITS IN THE HUMAN BODY.

1. Preheat the oven to 400°F. Line a baking sheet with parchment paper.

2. **MAKE THE PIZZA CRUST:** In a small bowl, stir together the flaxseed meal and ⅓ cup water and let sit for about 5 minutes to create a flax "egg."

3. In a food processor, combine the beans, flax egg, nutritional yeast, garlic, 1 teaspoon salt (use another ½ teaspoon if your beans were unsalted), and the cayenne and blend until smooth.

4. Spread the mixture onto the parchment paper in the shape of a pizza crust, about ⅛ inch thick. You'll fill most of the width of an 18 × 13-inch baking sheet.

5. Bake for 20 minutes. Carefully flip the crust (see Notes) to bake until the other side is totally dry, 15 to 20 minutes.

6. **MEANWHILE, MAKE THE TOPPING:** In a skillet, heat a bit of olive oil over medium heat. Add the shiitake mushrooms and onions and sauté until tender, about 20 minutes.

7. When the crust is done, top with the pizza sauce, vegan cheese, greens, squash, and mushrooms and onions. Return to the oven and bake for 10 minutes.

NOTES:
- To roast the squash, toss the slices with some olive oil, spread on a baking sheet, and roast for 30 minutes at 350°F.
- To flip the crust I place another sheet of parchment paper and another baking sheet over the one the crust is on, and using oven mitts, flip the sheets over. Then the crust will be on the new baking sheet. Slowly and carefully peel the original parchment off of the crust. Be careful not to break it!

Pure Comfort CARROT TUNA MELT

OG Black vegan restaurants always—*always*—have a carrot "tuna" on the menu. My favorite is the carrot tuna from Tassili's Raw here in Atlanta. This is my ode to that divine tuna, but in a comforting hot sandwich. For best results, use a great sourdough bread and your favorite vegan cheese on the melt. Elevate the vibes even more and serve it with the Cozy Chickpea Tomato Soup (page 131).

MAKES 4 SANDWICHES

2 medium carrots, peeled

1 (15.5-ounce) can chickpeas, drained and rinsed

⅓ cup vegan mayo

2 teaspoons Dijon mustard

2 teaspoons ume plum vinegar, plus more to taste

1 teaspoon celery seeds

2 teaspoons dulse seaweed flakes

3 sprigs fresh dill, minced

Kosher salt

Vegan stick butter or olive oil, for toasting the bread

8 slices sourdough bread

4 to 8 slices of your favorite vegan cheese

1. Preheat the oven to 375°F. Line a baking sheet with parchment paper.

2. Shred the carrots in the food processor using the fine shredding disc. Replace the attachment with the regular blade and pulse to mince.

3. Add the chickpeas, mayo, mustard, vinegar, celery seeds, dulse flakes, and dill to the processor and pulse until the chickpeas are chopped but still chunky. The texture should resemble tuna salad. Season to taste with salt and more ume plum vinegar.

4. Butter the slices of sourdough bread on both sides. Top 4 slices of bread with 1 or 2 slices of vegan cheese and a scoop of the chickpea/carrot mixture. Top off the sandwich with the other slice of bread.

5. Arrange on the baking sheet and bake until the bread is toasty and the cheese is starting to melt, about 10 minutes. Serve warm.

LOW-TECH CARROT TUNA MELT:

If you don't have a food processor, here's how to make the tuna mixture. Shred the carrots on the small holes of a box grater. Place the chickpeas in a bowl and mash with a fork. Stir in the carrots, vegan mayo, mustard, ume plum vinegar, celery seeds, dulse flakes, and dill. Season with more ume plum vinegar and salt to taste. The rest of the recipe is the same.

Curried
RED BEAN TACOS

When you're in a rush and low on fresh ingredients, curried red bean tacos are a great way to make use of those canned beans you have in your pantry. I often make these for my daughter, Jorji, on busy days during the week, when I want to prepare something quick, hot, and nourishing. Don't forget to finish with the salsa.

SERVES 4

CURRIED RED BEANS

- 1 tablespoon coconut oil or avocado oil
- 2 garlic cloves, minced
- 1 tablespoon curry powder
- 3 cups cooked red beans or kidney beans or 2 (15-ounce) cans, drained and rinsed
- 1 teaspoon sea salt, plus more to taste

TACOS

- 8 small corn tortillas (aka taco sliders) or 4 regular (5-inch) corn tortillas
- 1 cup baby spinach
- Peach Salsa (page 242)
- 1 avocado, sliced
- 1 jalapeño pepper, sliced, for garnish
- Lime wedges, for squeezing (optional)

1. **MAKE THE CURRIED RED BEANS:** In a skillet, warm the oil over medium-high heat. Add the garlic and sauté until it is fragrant and slightly golden, about 30 seconds. Add the curry powder and toast for 30 seconds.

2. Stir in the red beans, salt, and ¼ cup water. Cook over medium heat for 10 minutes.

3. Use a potato masher or fork to mash half of the beans. Add more water if necessary to soften the beans. Season with more salt to taste.

4. **ASSEMBLE THE TACOS:** Warm the corn tortillas in the microwave, on a gas stove, or in the oven. To warm them in the microwave: Wrap the tortillas in a damp paper towel and microwave for about 15 seconds until soft and hot. To warm them on the stove: Place them on the stove's gas flame. They'll soften and brown on the corners. Warm each side for about 10 seconds. To warm in the oven, preheat to 375°F. Place the tortillas directly onto the oven racks for 5 minutes. Keep the tortillas warm by wrapping them in a clean kitchen towel until ready to use.

5. Fill the warmed corn tortillas with a handful of spinach, topped with the curried red beans, peach salsa, avocado, and pepper.

6. Serve immediately with lime wedges, if using.

Tofu
SALMON

This is a recipe that I know I'll make for the rest of my life. I haven't had fish in years, but friends who have tell me it tastes just like fish, which makes me so happy! This dish is probably the most time-consuming in the book, and requires that you press the tofu and let it marinate for at least 6 hours, preferably overnight. But despite the pressing and marinating, it's easy to make. The briny flavors that emerge make it absolutely worth it, and I can assure you that your dinner guests will be over the moon.

MAKES 8 FILLETS (SERVES 4)

2 (14-ounce) blocks firm or extra-firm tofu

1 tablespoon mellow (white) miso

1 tablespoon capers

1 tablespoon caper brine

1 tablespoon tamari soy sauce

1 tablespoon ume plum vinegar or rice vinegar

1 small slice raw beet (to yield about 1 tablespoon when pureed)

2 teaspoons Better Than Bouillon vegetable base

Extra-virgin olive oil or oil spray

¼ cup cornstarch

2 sheets toasted nori, cut to fit the bottom of the tofu, or 8 sheets toasted snack nori

1. Press the tofu (see To Press Tofu, page 54) for at least 1 hour. Meanwhile, in a blender, combine the miso, capers, caper brine, tamari, vinegar, beet, bouillon base, and 1 cup water and blend until smooth.

2. Cut a block of tofu in half lengthwise and then cut each piece in half at a slight diagonal: Don't cut corner to corner; instead you want to end up with 2 triangle-ish pieces whose "noses" are no narrower than ½ inch. Repeat with the second block. The object is to get a piece shaped like a typical salmon fillet, which is thick at one end and thin at the other.

3. Flip the pieces so a sloping cut side is up. Use a paring knife to cut diagonal slits across the top of the tofu to resemble the texture of salmon. Don't cut more than ½ inch deep; doing so may cause your tofu to fall apart when handling. Repeat with all of the tofu and place in a dish. Depending on the size of your dish you may have to layer the tofu "fillets" on top of each other to fit.

4. Pour the marinade over the tofu, making sure all of the fillets are coated. Place in the fridge to marinate for at least 6 hours or overnight.

5. Preheat the oven to 350°F. Grease a 9 × 13-inch baking dish with olive oil.

6. Sprinkle half of the cornstarch onto a dinner plate. Remove a fillet from the marinade. Dip a piece of nori into the marinade to help it stick, then place it on the bottom of the tofu. Use your dry hand to gently dip the tofu in the cornstarch to coat each side. Place the tofu in the baking dish, nori-side up. Brush each side of the tofu with oil. Repeat for all the fillets. Refresh the plate with the remaining cornstarch when the first batch runs out.

7. Bake for 20 minutes. Flip and bake until the edges are crispy, another 15 minutes, before serving.

AIR-FRYER TOFU SALMON:

Prepare, marinate, and coat the tofu fillets as directed. Spray the bottom of the air-fryer basket with oil. Layer in the fillets, nori-side up, keeping at least 1 inch of space between them. Depending on the size of your air fryer, you may need to do this in batches. Cook at 350°F for 10 minutes. Flip and cook the second side for 10 minutes.

WHY EAT VEGAN SALMON, AND NOT THE REAL THING? WILD SALMON IS A CRUCIAL FOUNDATION OF THE NATIVE ECOSYSTEMS IN WHICH THEY ARE FOUND, PARTICULARLY THE NORTHERN PACIFIC. YET THEIR POPULATIONS ARE UNDER THREAT AND DECLINING. FARM-RAISED SALMON IS RIFE WITH PROBLEMS OF DISEASE, PARASITES, AND POLLUTION. THESE ISSUES OF OVERFISHING AND POLLUTION FROM FARM-RAISED FISH PLAGUE THE ENTIRE SEAFOOD INDUSTRY. BECAUSE OF THIS, AND OTHER REASONS, I CHOOSE PLANT-BASED ALTERNATIVES TO SEAFOOD.

Mushroom Carnitas TACOS

King oyster (aka trumpet) mushrooms can be shredded to create an incredible meaty and chewy texture. They are the best replacement for pulled pork in any recipe. Here the shredded mushrooms are braised in a citrus-based sauce, then caramelized under the broiler until the tops turn crispy. You can use young green jackfruit as a replacement for the mushrooms, but the experience is not the same. Look for king oyster mushrooms at an Asian grocery store. They're usually less than five dollars a pack.

SERVES 4

MUSHROOM CARNITAS

1 pound king oyster (trumpet) mushrooms

2 tablespoons grapeseed oil

½ yellow onion, diced

4 garlic cloves, minced

1 jalapeño pepper, seeded and minced

1 tablespoon dried oregano

2 teaspoons ground cumin

1 teaspoon sea salt, plus more to taste

1 teaspoon freshly ground black pepper

¼ cup freshly squeezed orange juice (about 1 small orange)

2 tablespoons fresh lime juice (about ½ lime)

1 tablespoon tamari soy sauce

TACOS

8 corn tortillas

2 avocados, sliced

1 cup shredded red cabbage

1 jalapeño pepper, thinly sliced

1 to 2 tomatoes, diced

Quickly Pickle-y Onions (recipe follows)

½ cup chopped fresh cilantro

Lime wedges, for squeezing

1. **MAKE THE MUSHROOM CARNITAS:** Cut the tough bottom inch off of the mushrooms, then use a fork to shred the entirety of the mushroom. The shreds should resemble pulled pork or chicken. Set aside.

2. Warm a large pot over medium heat. Add the oil and once the oil is warm, add the onions, garlic, and jalapeño and sauté until the onions are soft, about 3 minutes.

3. Stir in the mushrooms, oregano, cumin, salt, and pepper. Add the orange juice, lime juice, and soy sauce and stir again. Bring to a simmer over medium-low heat, cover, and cook until the mushrooms have reduced in size and are tender, about 30 minutes. Season to taste with more salt.

4. Preheat the broiler to low and line a baking sheet with parchment paper. Use a fork to lift the mushrooms out of the pot and the accumulated liquid and place on the baking sheet. Broil until the tops of the shredded mushrooms are crispy and browned, about 15 minutes.

5. **ASSEMBLE THE TACOS:** Warm the tortillas over a stovetop flame, in the microwave wrapped in a damp paper towel, or in the oven wrapped in aluminum foil.

6. Fill the tortillas with mushroom carnitas, avocado, red cabbage, jalapeño, tomatoes, pickled onions, cilantro, and a squeeze of lime juice.

QUICKLY PICKLE-Y ONIONS

Pickled onions are such an important condiment. You can use them to add tangy flavor to sandwiches, salads, avocado toast, and definitely tacos. Pickled onions will keep in the fridge for up to 2 weeks.

MAKES ½ PINT

1 cup apple cider vinegar

2 tablespoons cane sugar

1 teaspoon sea salt

1 large red onion, very thinly sliced

1. In a half-pint glass jar with a tight-fitting lid, combine the vinegar, sugar, and salt. Stir well until the sugar and salt dissolve. Add the sliced onions and press them down gently to cover completely with the pickling liquid. Secure the lid and set aside on the kitchen counter to pickle for at least 1 hour before using.

2. Store the onions in a tightly sealed glass jar in the refrigerator for up to 2 weeks.

Good & Dirty RICE

Dirty rice is a classic one-pot dish that Black Americans in Louisiana and other parts of the South have been preparing for generations. This is one of the few recipes where I use vegan "meat," to stay true to the original essence of the dish. Rooted in the African American tradition of using regional, inexpensive ingredients, you likely have most of what you need to make this peppery rice mixture in your pantry.

SERVES 6

2 tablespoons grapeseed oil or avocado oil

1 yellow onion, diced

1 green bell pepper, diced

2 celery stalks, diced

Sea salt

4 garlic cloves, minced

3 scallions, diced

10 ounces mushrooms, minced

1 bay leaf

½ pound vegan ground "meat"

1 cup veggie broth

½ teaspoon dried thyme

2 teaspoons porcini mushroom powder (optional)

2 tablespoons Creole seasoning, plus more to taste

5 cups cooked white rice

2 tablespoons soy sauce, plus more to taste

¼ cup chopped fresh parsley

Hot sauce, for serving

1. In a large skillet, warm the oil over medium heat. Add the onion, bell pepper, celery, and a pinch of salt and sauté until the vegetables begin to soften, about 3 minutes. Add the garlic and scallions and continue to cook until the onions are translucent, about 3 minutes.

2. Add the mushrooms and sauté until tender, 5 to 8 minutes. Add the bay leaf, vegan "meat," veggie broth, thyme, porcini powder, and Creole seasoning. Stir well and cook until the "meat" begins to brown, about 2 minutes. Depending on the type of vegan "meat" you are using, you may need to cook it a little longer. Stir in the cooked rice and soy sauce and cook for 5 minutes, making sure all of the rice is coated and dirty. Season to taste with more soy sauce or Creole seasoning.

3. Remove from the heat. Serve garnished with the fresh parsley and hot sauce for the table.

Korean Pulled 'Shroom SANDWICHES

Korean cuisine is among the best in the world, and despite what you might think based on your visits to Korean BBQ restaurants, there are many incredible plant-based dishes, too. Though I grew up with a lot of Korean friends, I didn't fall in love with the cuisine until I moved to New York and discovered Koreatown's Woorijip cafe. At least twice a week I'd pop in and grab lunch staples like veggie japchae, Korean fried rice, glazed sweet potato, and scallion pancakes. It was there that I first tasted gochujang, a sweet and savory red pepper paste made with fermented soybeans that literally tastes like an umami explosion in your mouth. Gochujang is a must in these Korean 'shroom sandwiches. You can find both spicy and mild versions of gochujang at Asian grocery stores, Whole Foods, or online.

These sandwiches are insanely yummy. Balance the heat by topping the pulled 'shrooms with the broccoli slaw. Take them to a cookout and watch the meat lovers fall in love.

MAKES 4 SANDWICHES

- 2 pounds king oyster (trumpet) mushrooms
- ¼ cup soy sauce
- 2 tablespoons cane sugar
- 1 tablespoon rice vinegar
- 1 tablespoon vegan gochujang (Korean chile paste)
- 1 tablespoon toasted sesame oil
- 2 garlic cloves, minced (about 1 tablespoon)
- 2 teaspoons minced or shredded fresh ginger
- ½ teaspoon freshly ground black pepper
- Broccoli Slaw (page 168)
- 4 vegan burger buns, toasted

1. Place a mushroom on the cutting board and slice off the tough bottom. Holding the mushroom with one hand, use your other hand to shred the mushroom lengthwise with a sturdy fork. Do this with each of the mushrooms and place the shredded pieces in a bowl.

2. In a small bowl, whisk together the soy sauce, sugar, rice vinegar, gochujang, sesame oil, garlic, ginger, and black pepper.

3. Pour the sauce over the mushrooms and toss well, making sure all of the mushrooms are coated. Set aside for 10 minutes.

4. Warm a skillet over medium-high heat. Reduce the heat to medium, add the shredded mushrooms, and cook, stirring occasionally, until the mushrooms are tender, about 20 minutes. Remove from the heat.

5. To assemble the sandwiches, add a scoop of broccoli slaw to the bottom half of each burger bun. Top with the hot shredded mushrooms and the top bun.

6. Serve hot.

BROCCOLI SLAW

I use this broccoli slaw to elevate the Korean Pulled 'Shroom Sandwiches (page 166), but honestly, this slaw is good enough to eat solo. Making broccoli slaw is a great way to use broccoli stems after you eat the flower tops. Broccoli stems have a crunchy texture and mild broccoli flavor.

SERVES 4

4 large broccoli stems, peeled and shredded

2 medium carrots, shredded (about 1 cup)

¼ cup diced red onion

¼ cup vegan mayo

1½ teaspoons Dijon mustard

1½ teaspoons fresh lemon juice

1½ teaspoons apple cider vinegar

1 teaspoon pure maple syrup or agave syrup

½ teaspoon sea salt, plus more to taste

½ teaspoon freshly ground black pepper

1. In a large bowl, toss together the shredded broccoli stems, carrot, and onion.

2. In a small bowl, mix together the mayo, mustard, lemon juice, vinegar, maple syrup, salt, and pepper. Add the dressing to the vegetables, stir well, and season with more salt to taste. Let marinate in the refrigerator for 1 hour before serving.

Black-Eyed Pea CURRY

The American South and South Asia link up in this delightful celebration of both regions' culinary offerings. Black-eyed peas are a staple of African American cuisine, often prepared for major holidays like New Year's, served as a side during family cookouts, and even baked into fritters and other snacks. This soothing curry dish, which can be prepared in the Instant Pot or on the stove, celebrates this wondrous legume, taking you on a nurturing journey through the rich, indulgent flavors of both parts of the world.

SERVES 4 TO 6

1 pound dried black-eyed peas

2 tablespoons coconut oil

2 teaspoons curry powder

1 teaspoon ground turmeric

1 teaspoon ground coriander

1 teaspoon ground cumin

1 teaspoon garam masala

3 to 5 garlic cloves, minced, to taste

1-inch knob fresh ginger, minced

1 red or yellow onion, diced

Sea salt

2 (14.5-ounce) cans diced fire-roasted tomatoes

1 (13.5-ounce) can full-fat coconut milk

2 cups water mixed with 2 teaspoons Better Than Bouillon vegetable base (or 2 cups vegetable broth), plus more water (or broth) as needed

2 sweet potatoes, peeled and cut into ½-inch cubes

2 teaspoons avocado oil

Freshly ground black pepper

FOR SERVING

White rice or Perfect Every Time Brown Rice (page 237)

Freshly ground black pepper

Chopped fresh cilantro

Lime wedges, for squeezing

1. In a large bowl, combine the black-eyed peas with water to cover. Soak for at least 6 hours. Drain well.

2. Preheat the oven to 375°F. Line a baking sheet with parchment paper.

3. In a large pot, warm the coconut oil over medium heat. Add the spices and toast until fragrant, about 30 seconds. Stir in the garlic and ginger and cook until the garlic is fragrant, about 30 seconds. Stir in the onion and a pinch of salt and cook until translucent, about 3 minutes.

4. Add the diced tomatoes, black-eyed peas, coconut milk, water with the bouillon base, and 1 teaspoon salt. Bring to a boil. Reduce to a simmer, partially cover, and cook until the beans are

continues ▶

continued ▶

tender, 40 to 45 minutes. Add more water or vegetable broth to thin if necessary.

5. While the beans cook, toss the cubed sweet potatoes with the avocado oil. Spread out on the lined baking sheet and sprinkle with ½ teaspoon salt. Roast until tender, about 35 minutes.

6. Stir the roasted sweet potatoes into the finished black-eyed peas. Season to taste with black pepper and more salt.

7. Serve with rice and garnish with black pepper and cilantro. Serve with lime wedges.

INSTANT POT BLACK-EYED PEA CURRY:

1. Soak and drain the black-eyed peas as directed.

2. Preheat the oven and roast the sweet potatoes as directed.

3. Turn the Instant Pot to Sauté on high and add the coconut oil. Add the spices and toast until fragrant, about 30 seconds. Stir in the garlic and ginger and cook until the garlic is fragrant, about 30 seconds. Stir in the onions and a pinch of salt and cook until translucent, about 3 minutes. Cancel the Sauté setting.

4. Add the diced tomatoes, black-eyed peas, coconut milk, and 1 teaspoon salt. (Note that no water with bouillon base is added to this version.) Seal the lid and pressure cook for 25 minutes. Let the pressure release naturally (or if you are in a hurry, allow it to natural pressure release for at least 10 minutes).

5. Stir in the roasted sweet potatoes. Season to taste with black pepper and more salt.

6. Serve as directed.

Teriyaki Tempeh TACOS

I've learned that, by and large, following Nana's lead is the way to go in life. So when she shared her recipe for teriyaki tempeh tacos, I knew I had to add them to my weekly menu. Tempeh, a fermented soybean cake from Indonesia, is a terrific source of protein that you can cook in numerous ways. Here it's marinated in a sweet-and-sour teriyaki sauce and nestled inside a flaky corn tortilla. I bet you've already got your apron out, don't you?

SERVES 4

TERIYAKI TEMPEH

1 tablespoon coconut oil or avocado oil

1½ tablespoons minced fresh ginger

3 garlic cloves, minced

½ cup soy sauce

3 tablespoons rice vinegar

1 teaspoon toasted sesame oil

1 tablespoon pure maple syrup

1 tablespoon coconut sugar or brown sugar (light or dark)

1 tablespoon arrowroot powder or cornstarch

2 (8-ounce) packages tempeh, diced

TACOS

8 corn tortillas

Mango Guacamole (page 245)

Shredded red cabbage

Jalapeño pepper, sliced (optional)

Chopped fresh cilantro

Lime wedges, for squeezing

1. **MAKE THE TERIYAKI TEMPEH:** In a medium saucepan, warm the coconut oil over medium heat. Add the ginger, garlic, soy sauce, rice vinegar, sesame oil, maple syrup, and coconut sugar and bring to a gentle simmer.

2. In a small bowl, combine ⅓ cup water with the arrowroot and stir well to break up any chunks. Slowly pour the arrowroot slurry into the simmering sauce and stir.

3. Add the diced tempeh to the sauce, cover, and cook over medium-low heat until the tempeh is tender and has soaked up the flavor from the sauce, about 20 minutes.

4. **ASSEMBLE THE TACOS:** Warm the tortillas over a stovetop flame, in the microwave wrapped in a damp paper towel, or in the oven. To warm in the oven, preheat to 375°F. Place the tortillas directly onto the oven racks for 5 minutes. Keep the tortillas warm by wrapping them in a clean kitchen towel until ready to use.

5. Top the tortillas with tempeh, mango guacamole, shredded red cabbage, peppers (if using), and fresh cilantro. Serve with lime wedges.

Za'atar Cauliflower STEAKS

There are lots of ways to enjoy this cauliflower steak. You can make it the centerpiece of a dinner, or serve it as a side. You'll notice that when you're prepping the cauliflower steaks, some pieces will fall off. Simply place any extra bits on top of the intact cauliflower steaks before or after roasting.

SERVES 4

1 medium head cauliflower, leaves removed

3 tablespoons extra-virgin olive oil

¼ cup tahini

2 tablespoons fresh lemon juice

½ cup panko bread crumbs

2 tablespoons fine dried bread crumbs

1 tablespoon za'atar seasoning

1 teaspoon garlic powder

½ teaspoon smoked paprika

½ teaspoon sea salt

Assorted minced fresh herbs, for serving

1. Preheat the oven to 375°F. Line a baking sheet with parchment paper.

2. Cut the cauliflower lengthwise through the core into four ¾-inch steaks. Arrange the cauliflower steaks evenly on the baking sheet and place any extra pieces on top of the cauliflower slices.

3. Put 2 tablespoons of the olive oil in a small bowl and use a kitchen brush to grease the tops of each cauliflower steak. (Alternatively, you can grease the tops with olive oil spray.)

4. In another bowl, whisk together the tahini, 2 tablespoons water, and the lemon juice until creamy. Spoon some of the tahini sauce over the top of each cauliflower steak and spread evenly.

5. In another bowl (or the same one you used for the tahini), combine the remaining 1 tablespoon oil, the panko, fine bread crumbs, za'atar, garlic powder, smoked paprika, and salt. Stir well, then spoon the crunchy topping over each cauliflower steak and spread evenly to coat the tops well.

6. Bake until the cauliflower is tender and the topping slightly golden and crispy, 35 to 40 minutes.

7. Serve hot sprinkled with minced fresh herbs.

Mushroom Bulgogi LETTUCE CUPS

While my daughter, Jorji, loves helping me slice mushrooms, she's rarely a fan of the fungi itself. She totally loves these mushroom bulgogi lettuce cups, though, and I think it has something to do with the soy sauce–marinated mushrooms, not to mention the super-fun shape of the cups. Use lion's mane mushrooms if you can find them, but if you can't, oyster, maitake, and even cremini mushrooms work great as well. Though they appear to be cute little bites (and they are, indeed, quite cute), these savory cups are pretty hearty, and can easily be a side, hors d'oeuvre, or full meal.

MAKES 8 LETTUCE CUPS (SERVES 4)

MARINATED MUSHROOMS

- 1 pound lion's mane mushrooms, pulled apart into 4-inch pieces, or other type of mushroom, thinly sliced
- ¼ cup plus 2 tablespoons dark soy sauce
- ¼ cup toasted sesame oil
- 2 tablespoons mirin
- 1 tablespoon cane sugar
- 1 cup grated Asian pear or firm Anjou pear (about 1 pear)
- 6 garlic cloves, minced
- 2 teaspoons grated fresh ginger
- 4 teaspoons sesame seeds
- 1 teaspoon freshly ground black pepper

ASSEMBLY

- 1 tablespoon toasted sesame oil
- 8 Bibb lettuce leaves
- 2 cups cooked rice
- 2 scallions, green tops only, sliced, for garnish
- Sesame seeds, for garnish

1. **MARINATE THE MUSHROOMS:** Place the mushroom pieces into a large bowl. In another bowl, combine the soy sauce, sesame oil, the mirin, sugar, Asian pear, garlic, ginger, sesame seeds, and black pepper and stir well. Pour over the mushrooms and toss well to coat—you may want to use your hands for this. Let the mushrooms marinate for 20 minutes.

2. **ASSEMBLE THE BULGOGI:** In a large skillet, warm the sesame oil over medium-high heat. Add the mushrooms and marinade and stir. Arrange the mushrooms in the skillet in an even layer, place a heavy lid or bacon press directly onto the mushrooms, and cook this way for 10 minutes. Stir and continue to cook, stirring occasionally, until the mushrooms are tender yet meaty, about 10 minutes.

3. Fill the Bibb lettuce leaves with rice and top with mushroom bulgogi. Garnish with scallion greens and a sprinkling of sesame seeds.

Lion's Mane
CRAB CAKES

My dad is from D.C., so I grew up eating crabs and incredible Maryland crab cakes. To make a vegan crab cake that would make my Chesapeake family proud, I use lion's mane mushrooms. Lion's mane looks like a fuzzy white puff ball and is celebrated for its anticancer and cognitive health benefits. It has a delightful pillowy texture that turns delicate yet meaty when cooked. Shredded lion's mane mushroom has a light and flaky texture like crabmeat.

Briny ume plum vinegar and dulse seaweed make it taste like the sea. And it would not be a crab cake without Old Bay seasoning.

SERVES 4

2 lion's mane mushrooms, hand-shredded into small pieces (about 2½ cups)

½ cup plus 2 tablespoons panko bread crumbs or crushed saltine crackers

½ cup vegan mayo

1 tablespoon Old Bay seasoning (use less if using saltine crumbs)

½ jalapeño pepper, seeded and minced

2 tablespoons minced fresh dill

1 teaspoon dulse seaweed flakes

1 teaspoon ume plum vinegar

1 cup avocado oil or olive oil

Fresh herbs, for garnish

Garlic Lemon Aioli (recipe follows), for garnish

Lemon slices, for garnish (optional)

1. In a large bowl, combine the shredded lion's mane mushrooms, panko, mayo, Old Bay, jalapeño, dill, dulse flakes, and vinegar. Stir well to thoroughly mix.

2. Dampen your hands and form the mixture into tight cakes, using about ½ cup per cake. Set on a plate until ready to fry.

3. Line a large plate with paper towels and set near the stove. In a large skillet, heat the oil over medium-high heat. Test the oil by adding a tiny speck of the batter to make sure it is hot before adding the crab cakes.

4. Add 3 to 4 cakes to the hot oil (depending on the size of your pan) and cook until golden brown and crispy on both sides, about 5 minutes per side. Transfer the cooked crab cakes to the paper towels to drain. Repeat with the remaining cakes.

5. Serve the crab cakes hot, garnished with fresh herbs, aioli, and lemon slices (if using).

GARLIC LEMON AIOLI

MAKES ½ CUP AIOLI

1 garlic bulb

1 teaspoon extra-virgin olive oil or avocado oil

½ cup vegan mayo

1 tablespoon fresh lemon juice

1 teaspoon lemon zest, plus more to taste

½ teaspoon cane sugar

1. Preheat the oven to 400°F.

2. Cut off the top of the bulb of garlic, so that the cloves are visible. Place the garlic bulb cut-side up onto a small sheet of aluminum foil. Drizzle the oil over the cut side of the garlic and wrap the foil around the garlic to cover completely. Place in the oven and roast for 45 minutes. The garlic cloves should be fragrant, tender, and golden. Allow the garlic to cool until safe to handle.

3. Squeeze the roasted garlic cloves out of the bulb and straight into a small food processor. Add the vegan mayo, lemon juice, lemon zest, and sugar to the food processor, and blend until smooth. Add more lemon zest to taste. Serve the aioli immediately, or store in the fridge for up to 5 days.

West African
NUT STEW

When my daughter, JJ, was just a few days old, my friend Brandi Sellers brought me a batch of her West African peanut stew, and my life was changed forever. Also known as "groundnut stew," the dish is a staple of West and Central African cuisine, and while recipes vary widely, there's almost always a heavenly spice blend of black pepper, paprika, cumin, and other spices to amplify the nutty taste of the smooth, creamy peanut paste. Peanut allergies are common, which is why I use sunflower seed or almond butter in my version, but you could use peanut butter if it's not a problem; it'll be delicious either way. Take care not to overcook your vegetables—you want tender bites of potatoes and greens that'll be saturated in the smooth, nutty stew.

SERVES 4

- 2 tablespoons extra-virgin olive oil or avocado oil
- 1 medium red or yellow onion, diced
- 3 garlic cloves, minced
- 2-inch knob fresh ginger, minced
- 1 red bell pepper, diced
- ½ jalapeño pepper, seeded and diced
- Sea salt
- 1 tablespoon ground cumin
- 1 teaspoon coriander seeds
- 1 medium sweet potato, peeled and cut into ½-inch cubes

- 1 Yukon Gold potato or red potato, cut into ½-inch cubes
- 1 (14.5-ounce) can diced tomatoes or 3 fresh tomatoes, diced
- 4 to 6 cups water or vegetable broth
- 1 (20-ounce) can young green jackfruit chunks, drained and halved
- 1½ cups cooked kidney beans or 1 (15-ounce) can, drained and rinsed
- 1½ tablespoons Better Than Bouillon vegetable base (omit if using veggie broth)

- 2 teaspoons smoked paprika
- 1 tablespoon harissa paste (optional)
- ½ to 1 cup sunflower seed butter or nut butter, such as almond or peanut
- 1 bunch collard greens, sliced into thin ribbons (removing the stems is optional since you're cutting them so thin)

FOR SERVING

Cooked rice

Freshly ground black pepper

Chopped fresh cilantro

Lime wedges, for squeezing

1. In a large pot, warm the oil over medium-high heat. Add the onion, garlic, ginger, bell pepper, jalapeño, and a pinch of salt and sauté until the onions are translucent, about 3 minutes.

2. Stir in the cumin and coriander and cook until fragrant, about 30 seconds or so. Add the sweet potato, Yukon Gold potato, tomatoes, water, jackfruit, and beans. Bring to a simmer and add the bouillon base. Partially cover and cook until the potatoes are tender but not mushy, about 20 minutes.

3. Stir in the smoked paprika and harissa (if using). Stir in ½ cup of the sunflower seed butter. Add up to another ½ cup if you'd like it very thick. Season with 1 teaspoon salt. Add the collard greens and cook until they are bright green and tender, about 5 minutes.

4. Season to taste with more salt.

5. Serve over rice and garnish with black pepper and cilantro. Serve with lime wedges.

Parsnip Carrot CURRY

There's nothing like a comforting bowl of curry during the cool months of fall and winter. When the temperatures drop below 45°F I start craving this parsnip carrot curry. Parsnips aren't usually associated with South Asian–inspired curry, but I really love their sweet, earthy flavor married to fragrant spices. Root vegetables are especially nourishing and rich in minerals like potassium. Serve this curry over the Perfect Every Time Brown Rice (page 237) and with the Beet Lime Chutney (page 87).

SERVES 4

1 tablespoon extra-virgin olive oil

¼ teaspoon mustard seeds

2 tablespoons curry powder (I use sambar masala)

2 dried chile peppers, crushed

½ yellow onion, diced

3 garlic cloves, minced

3 parsnips, peeled and cut into ½-inch cubes

3 carrots, peeled and cut into ½-inch cubes

¼ vegetable bouillon cube

1 cup full-fat coconut milk

1. In a large deep pot, heat the olive oil over medium heat. Add the mustard seeds, 1 tablespoon of the curry powder, and the crushed chiles and fry for 30 seconds. Add the onion and garlic, stir to coat, and cook until the onion is translucent, about 3 minutes. Add the parsnips, carrots, and bouillon cube.

2. Stir well, cover, and cook for 5 minutes. Add the coconut milk and the remaining 1 tablespoon curry powder. Cover and bring to a boil. Uncover and simmer until the vegetables are tender, though not too mushy, and the coconut milk has thickened, leaving a creamy sauce, about 20 minutes.

Simple OYSTER MUSHROOM STEAKS

Use any flavorful mushroom for this recipe; because of their natural flavor, you don't need a lot of spice. Oyster mushrooms are most common, but I also like using maitakes. Serve these mushrooms with Perfect Pea Pesto Pasta (page 185), curry, over salad, or with Roasted Grape Bulgur Pilaf (page 150). The trick to making the meatiest mushrooms is to cook them over medium to medium-low heat and press them with something heavy while they cook. The best option is a bacon press, but even I don't have one. I usually use a flat lid from one of my pans or place my cast-iron skillet over them (not as easy to clean after). Pressing mushrooms draws out their liquids, concentrates the flavor, and gives them a meatier texture.

SERVES 4

- 2 pounds oyster or maitake mushrooms
- 1 tablespoon extra-virgin olive oil
- 2 garlic cloves, minced
- ½ teaspoon sea salt, plus more to taste
- ½ teaspoon freshly ground black pepper
- Minced fresh parsley, for serving
- Lemon wedges, for squeezing

1. Cut the tough bottom portion off of the mushrooms and brush clean with a damp paper towel or kitchen towel. Leave the mushrooms whole for meaty steaks, or cut them into smaller pieces for mushrooms with a little more crispiness.

2. In a skillet, heat the oil over medium heat. Add the garlic and sauté until slightly golden, about 1 minute. Be very careful not to burn the garlic.

3. Sprinkle the mushrooms with the salt and place gill-side up or cap-side down in the hot skillet. Place a bacon press, heavy skillet, or heavy pot lid directly onto the mushrooms and cook for 10 minutes over medium-low heat.

4. Flip the mushrooms, press again, and cook until the mushrooms are browned, tender, and juicy, 5 to 10 minutes.

5. Season with the pepper and more salt to taste.

6. Serve with minced fresh parsley and a squeeze of lemon.

Perfect
PEA PESTO PASTA

Traditionally made with pine nuts, garlic, basil leaves, and Parmigiano-Reggiano, pesto gets a vegan rebrand in this recipe. That sharp, distinct flavor associated with the pesto shines ever brighter, thanks to the addition of white miso, lemon juice, green peas, and a healthy amount of the freshest mint you can get your hands on (if you don't have fresh mint, up the amount of basil to make sure the dish maintains its herby essence). If you don't have any herbs, fresh spinach is the next best thing.

I like to serve this pasta topped with my Simple Oyster Mushroom Steaks (page 183), which add a perfect punch of umami. This reinvention of the Genovese favorite takes center stage at family brunches and dinner parties. Amazing alliteration paired with an unforgettable taste? It doesn't get much better than this, folks!

SERVES 4

2 tablespoons kosher salt

8 ounces gemelli, or your favorite short or long pasta

2 cups frozen green peas, plus more for garnish (optional)

1 cup fresh basil leaves, plus more for garnish (optional)

½ cup fresh mint leaves

2 tablespoons nutritional yeast

1 tablespoon mellow (white) miso

1 tablespoon fresh lemon juice

1 large garlic clove, peeled but whole

1 teaspoon sea salt, plus more to taste

¼ cup extra-virgin olive oil

Freshly ground black pepper

1. Bring a pot of water to a boil for the pasta and add the kosher salt. Add the pasta and cook to al dente according to the package directions.

2. Meanwhile, steam or microwave the peas until they are bright green and thawed: about 3 minutes if steaming. If microwaving, follow the directions on the bag.

3. Transfer the peas to a food processor along with the basil, mint, nutritional yeast, miso, lemon juice, garlic, and sea salt. Pulse to combine. With the machine running, pour in the olive oil and blend until creamy. The pesto can be as thin or chunky as you'd like, as long as all of the ingredients are well mixed.

4. Drain the pasta and return it to the pot. Toss with the pea pesto. Season to taste with sea salt and black pepper and garnish with basil and peas, if desired. Serve hot.

Thai Taste
TOFU STIR-FRY

This tofu stir-fry is inspired by my time in Thailand in 2011. I spent two months exploring the country, eating Thai regional cuisine, and taking cooking classes. This dish is an amalgamation of all the wonderful people I met and cooked with all those years ago, and true to what they taught me, I encourage you to make this colorful dish your own. Feel free to swap out the vegetables for whatever floats your boat, and adjust the spice level to what works best for you.

SERVES 4

1 (14-ounce) block extra-firm tofu, cut into ½-inch cubes

2 teaspoons plus 2 tablespoons toasted sesame oil

1 teaspoon sea salt

1 teaspoon garlic powder

¼ cup almond butter or peanut butter

¼ cup fresh lime juice

¼ cup soy sauce

1 tablespoon pure maple syrup or other liquid sweetener

½ yellow onion, thinly sliced

½ red bell pepper, thinly sliced

1 Thai chile pepper or ½ jalapeño pepper, minced (optional)

2 garlic cloves, minced

1-inch knob fresh ginger, minced or grated

1 cup thinly sliced red cabbage

1 cup chopped broccoli

Perfect Every Time Brown Rice (page 237), for serving

½ cup loosely packed chopped fresh cilantro

¼ cup toasted almonds or peanuts, chopped

Lime wedges, for squeezing

1. Preheat the oven to 375°F (see Note). Line a baking sheet with parchment paper.

2. In a bowl, toss the tofu with 2 teaspoons of the sesame oil, the salt, and garlic powder. Spread evenly onto the lined baking sheet and bake until golden and crispy, about 30 minutes.

3. In a small bowl, whisk together the almond butter, ⅔ cup water, the lime juice, soy sauce, and maple syrup. Set aside.

4. In a skillet with a lid, heat the remaining 2 tablespoons sesame oil over medium-high heat. Add the onion, bell pepper, chile pepper (if using), garlic, and ginger and sauté until the onions start to become translucent, about 3 minutes.

5. Add the red cabbage and broccoli and toss and sauté for 3 minutes.

6. Pour in the almond sauce and stir well. It may be slightly chunky when added but it will become creamy as it is stirred and heats. Cover the skillet and cook until the broccoli and cabbage are tender and bright, 5 to 10 minutes.

7. Remove from the heat, add the crispy tofu, and stir well. Serve over brown rice. Garnish with the fresh cilantro, chopped nuts, and lime wedges.

AIR-FRYER THAI TASTE TOFU STIR-FRY:

If you have an air fryer, this is the perfect place to use it. Preheat the air fryer to 375°F. Season the tofu as directed. Pour it into the basket of the air fryer and air-fry for 20 minutes, stirring halfway through.

DIVINE DESSERTS

My philosophy on desserts is, when you maintain a healthy way of eating that is low in sugar and processed foods, you can occasionally indulge in a decadent treat without any guilt. I don't go out of my way to create desserts that are filled with zero-calorie sweeteners, or hacked to pieces with "healthier swaps." In this chapter you're going to drool over Miso Caramel-y Banana Pudding (page 192), Sweet Potato Double-Chocolate Muffins (page 195), Blueberry Cornmeal Cookies (page 199), and Chocolate Pecan Pie (page 206), just to name a few. None of which are healthy, and that's 100 percent okay. Just don't plan on eating any of these on a daily basis. I adore rich and sugary desserts, but find that they taste so much better when I only eat them on special occasions.

Unless it comes in the form of fruit, sugar is sugar. Maple syrup and agave aren't really any healthier than cane sugar, but eaten in moderation, all can be part of an overall healthy and balanced diet. I avoid baking with zero-calorie sweeteners—even the natural ones like monk fruit and stevia—for a few reasons: For one, monk fruit and stevia do not have the same chemical composition as sugar, so they don't produce the same texture in baked goods. Secondly, in high amounts, these zero-calorie sweeteners have an aftertaste. Third, there is some evidence to suggest that regular consumption of zero-calorie sweeteners may make you crave more sweets. I don't mind using modest amounts of stevia, monk fruit, and erythritol in beverages like tea, but I avoid them in baking.

If you're one of those people who like to enjoy a sweet treat every day, I also have some healthy dessert options for you made with wholesome ingredients like fresh fruits, nuts, and whole grains. One of my favorites is the No-Bake Cherry Walnut Crumble (page 209).

Miso Caramel-y
BANANA PUDDING

I like to think of this as an extra-gourmet banana pudding. The savory miso goes so well with caramel, creating an absolutely lovely blend of sweet and salty. Banana pudding is, indeed, a comfort dessert, and this one is no exception. The vanilla pudding requires a few hours to set, so you'll want to plan ahead if serving it to guests. I recommend making this the day before, both to let the flavors set and so you aren't stressed on the day of a big event or dinner. This recipe will make a little more miso caramel than you need. That's strategic; it lasts for weeks and is sublime as a fruit or pretzel dip, or drizzled over ice cream.

SERVES 4

MISO CARAMEL

1 cup cane sugar

6 tablespoons vegan stick butter

2 tablespoons mellow (white) miso

3 tablespoons plain unsweetened oat milk

½ teaspoon sea salt

VANILLA PUDDING

2 cups plain unsweetened oat milk or other nondairy milk

2 tablespoons cane sugar or agave syrup

1½ tablespoons cornstarch or arrowroot powder

1 teaspoon pure vanilla extract

ASSEMBLY

30 vegan vanilla wafer cookies, plus more if needed

4 firm-ripe bananas, sliced

Vegan whipped cream

1. **MAKE THE MISO CARAMEL:** In a small saucepan, heat the sugar over medium heat until it becomes liquid, 10 to 15 minutes depending on your pan. At first the sugar will start to look slightly wet like sand, then it will clump as the sugars on the bottom liquefy. Stir the sugar every few minutes and be patient; it will become syrup soon.

2. When the sugar is liquid, remove it from the heat and add the vegan butter. It will bubble at first and then settle as you stir. Once the bubbling settles, add the miso. Use a whisk or fork to break up any chunks of miso as you stir.

3. Once smooth, gently stir in the oat milk and salt. Continue stirring until you have a smooth and creamy consistency. It will look thinner than you'd expect at first, but will thicken significantly as it cools. Transfer the caramel to a heatproof glass container and set aside to cool completely.

4. **MAKE THE VANILLA PUDDING:** In a small saucepan, heat 1½ cups of the oat milk and the sugar over medium heat. As it warms on the stove, mix the remaining ½ cup oat milk with the cornstarch in a small bowl. Whisk until smooth.

5. When the oat milk begins to simmer, reduce the heat to low and add the cornstarch mixture. Stir it gently until it begins to thicken. Remove from the heat and stir in the vanilla.

NOTE: I like to have at least four layers, so a tall 8-inch round dish is usually ideal for layering. You could even make individual servings by layering the ingredients in glass jars or cups.

6. Pour the pudding into a heatproof container and set aside to cool and thicken. Once it's at room temperature, I usually place it in the fridge for another hour or so. Two hours should be enough time for the pudding to set fully.

7. **ASSEMBLE THE BANANA PUDDING:** In your favorite glass dish or baking dish (see Note), assemble layers of vanilla cookies, banana slices, vanilla pudding, and miso caramel. Top with whipped cream, cookies, and miso caramel.

Sweet Potato DOUBLE-CHOCOLATE MUFFINS

Chocolate muffins like you've never had them. The secret for perfectly moist vegan muffins: almond flour. Sweet potato adds sweet complexity, and also contributes to the moistness and airiness of these muffins. Perhaps my favorite thing about these muffins is that the batter produces glossy muffin tops that are crispy along the edges and fluffy inside.

MAKES 12 MUFFINS

1 tablespoon ground flaxseed meal

1 cup spelt flour or whole-wheat pastry flour

1 cup almond flour

½ cup cane sugar

½ cup coconut sugar or light brown sugar

½ cup unsweetened cocoa powder

1 teaspoon baking soda

½ teaspoon sea salt

1 cup plain unsweetened soy milk or other nondairy milk

1 tablespoon apple cider vinegar

½ cup mashed sweet potato (see Note)

1 teaspoon pure vanilla extract

½ cup avocado oil

¼ cup chopped dark baking chocolate or vegan chocolate chips

IF YOU WANT TO MAKE THESE MUFFINS A LITTLE HEALTHIER, REDUCE THE SUGARS TO ⅓ CUP EACH, AND THE OIL TO ¼ CUP.

1. Preheat the oven to 400°F. Line 12 cups of a muffin tin with paper liners.

2. In a small bowl, mix the flaxseed meal with 2 tablespoons water. Set the mixture aside to thicken to create a flax "egg."

3. In a medium bowl, stir together the spelt flour, almond flour, cane sugar, coconut sugar, the cocoa, baking soda, and salt.

4. In another bowl, whisk together the soy milk, vinegar, flax egg, mashed sweet potato, vanilla, and oil.

5. Pour the soy milk mixture into the flour mixture and stir. Careful not to overmix. Fold in the chocolate chips.

6. Spoon the batter into the muffin cups. They will probably reach the top of the cups. That's great!

7. Bake until a toothpick inserted in the center of a muffin comes out clean, 25 to 30 minutes.

8. Allow to cool in the pan for 10 to 15 minutes before eating!

NOTE: Microwave or bake an 8-ounce sweet potato. Peel and finely mash the sweet potato and measure out ½ cup. (If you happen to watch the YouTube video for this recipe, I say ¼ cup, but I meant ½ cup.)

Georgia Peach
ICE CREAM

This ice cream tastes like my home state, Georgia. Growing up in a region where figs, peaches, and pecans are abundant, I learned that the three make a pretty fantastic bowl of ice cream. I roast the fruit to caramelize their sugars and add depth to the sweet flavor. If you don't have great figs, swap them out for two sweet peaches. Just make sure to roast the fruit before adding it to your ice cream maker.

MAKES 1 PINT

2½ cups full-fat coconut milk

½ cup cane sugar

Pinch of sea salt

1 teaspoon pure vanilla extract

2 peaches (unpeeled), finely chopped

5 fresh figs, stemmed and finely chopped

1½ teaspoons melted coconut oil

½ cup pecans

1. Preheat the oven to 400°F.

2. In a small saucepan, combine the coconut milk, sugar, and salt and warm over medium heat until the temperature reaches 160°F (or just until it starts to simmer). Stir well to make sure the sugar dissolves. Remove from the heat and stir in the vanilla. Transfer to a container and refrigerate for at least 8 hours.

3. In a medium bowl, toss the chopped peaches and figs with the coconut oil. Spread evenly in a baking dish. Spread the pecans in another baking dish.

4. Transfer both to the oven and toast the pecans for 6 minutes. Roast the fruit until soft, about 20 minutes.

5. Set the pecans aside at room temperature. Allow the peaches and figs to cool completely and refrigerate alongside the ice cream base.

6. When the fruit and ice cream base are well chilled, add them to an ice cream maker and churn according to the manufacturer's instructions. In the last 5 minutes of churning, add the pecans.

7. Place the churned ice cream into a freezer-safe container and set in the freezer to solidify for at least 2 hours.

8. Enjoy!

Blueberry Cornmeal COOKIES

Parents, I get it. Receiving a letter that you need to make baked goods that can serve twenty-five children and adults while you're in the middle of your ninth Zoom call of the day can be . . . daunting. But we know our teachers need our support, and I'm overjoyed to help them out and pitch in with school activities. True story: My daughter's pre-K teachers and admin staff still request these cookies!

Coconut oil gives these delicious cookies their buttery flavor, flaxseed meal creates an irresistible chew, and the kiddos go wild for the blue and yellow color from the beautiful (and healthy!) combination of blueberry and cornmeal.

MAKES TWELVE 4-INCH COOKIES

2 tablespoons ground flaxseed meal

½ cup coconut oil

½ cup packed light brown sugar

½ cup cane sugar

1 teaspoon pure vanilla extract

1½ cups all-purpose flour

½ cup fine grind cornmeal

1 teaspoon baking powder

½ teaspoon sea salt

½ cup blueberries, fresh or frozen (not thawed)

1. Preheat the oven to 350°F. Line a baking sheet with parchment paper.

2. In a small bowl, combine the flaxseed meal and ¼ cup water. Stir well and set aside to thicken for at least 5 minutes to create a flax "egg."

3. In a stand mixer fitted with the whisk, cream together the coconut oil and both sugars. Add the flax egg and vanilla and beat until combined.

4. Remove the bowl from the mixer base. Sift in the flour, cornmeal, baking powder, and salt. Use a rubber spatula or wooden spoon to mix the ingredients together. Once combined, add the blueberries. This dough is pretty dry, so you may want to use your hands to bring it all together. Careful not to overwork it.

5. Scoop the dough—about ¼ cup for large cookies and 2 tablespoons for smaller cookies—and form into balls. Arrange 6 cookies on the baking sheet, leaving 2 inches between them so they have room to spread. Press the cookies about ½-inch flat with greased fingers or the bottom of a measuring cup.

6. Bake until fragrant and golden around the edges, about 16 minutes for large cookies and 13 minutes for small.

7. Let them cool on the pan for 5 minutes before transferring them to a wire rack. Let them cool for at least 10 minutes before eating.

8. Repeat with the remaining dough using the same parchment paper.

Perfect
PEACH PIE

When I was my daughter Jorji's age, I wasn't the biggest fan of fruit pies. Now, I've learned how to utilize the sweetness of fruit, rather than sugar, to make a truly wonderful pie. Use the best peaches you can get for this pie. And by "best" fruit I don't mean unblemished. Scratch-and-dent peaches from the farmers' market are cheap and exceptional. Imperfections, in produce and in life, are to be celebrated! It's okay if it's shaped in an unusual way; and smaller produce is often tastier. A little overripe is perfect for this pie, though of course you should avoid buying moldy or rotten peaches.

MAKES ONE 9-INCH PIE

Double-Crust Pie Dough (page 203)

8 ripe yellow peaches, peeled (see Notes, page 202) and sliced (about 4½ cups)

¼ cup plus 2 tablespoons cane sugar

¼ cup packed brown sugar (dark or light)

3 tablespoons cornstarch

¼ teaspoon freshly grated nutmeg

¼ teaspoon ground cinnamon

¼ teaspoon ground cardamom

⅛ teaspoon sea salt

2 teaspoons fresh lemon juice

1 tablespoon vegan stick butter

Wash: 2 tablespoons nondairy milk mixed with 1 teaspoon pure maple syrup

1. Make and chill the pie dough as directed. When ready to make the pie, take one of the dough balls out to warm up for at least 10 minutes before rolling out.

2. Place the dough ball on a flour-dusted smooth stone surface (if you don't have a stone surface use parchment paper). Use a floured rolling pin to roll the dough into a round about ⅛ inch thick and 12 inches in diameter. Fit the round of dough into a 9-inch pie dish. Trim the dough to a scant 1 inch of overhang (do not crimp yet). Set the pie shell in the refrigerator.

3. In a bowl, toss the peach slices with both sugars. Stir well and set aside for 1 hour.

4. Reserving the liquid, drain the peaches. Set the peaches aside, but have the liquid at the ready.

5. Preheat the oven to 400°F.

6. Bring out the second ball of dough and let it sit for 10 minutes before rolling out.

7. Meanwhile, in a small saucepan, combine the cornstarch, nutmeg, cinnamon, cardamom, and salt. Set over medium heat and slowly pour in the peach liquid, whisking as you pour to break up any clumps. Bring to a simmer and continue whisking until it has thickened, about 2 minutes. If it thickens too much, add 2 to 4 tablespoons water.

8. Remove from the heat and stir in the lemon juice and vegan butter. Fold in the sliced peaches.

continues ▶

continued ▶

9. Roll the second dough ball out to ⅛ inch thick and about 12 inches in diameter. With a sharp knife, cut the dough into strips 1 inch wide.

10. Bring the pie shell out of the refrigerator and pour the peaches into the shell. Use the dough strips to make a lattice top (see Notes), and crimp the edges of the pie shell and the lattice together tightly to seal.

11. Brush the lattice top and edges with the milk/maple syrup wash, then cover the edges with aluminum foil.

12. Bake until the crust is lightly browned, about 50 minutes.

13. Allow the pie to cool for 1 hour or so before serving. Allow it to cool completely or refrigerate for a less messy filling.

NOTES:

TO PEEL PEACHES: Set up a big bowl of ice and water and have it near the stove. Bring a large saucepan of water to a boil. Cut an "X" in the bottom of each peach. Place the peaches in the boiling water (as many as can fit in the pan) and blanch until the skins begin to darken, about 30 to 60 seconds. With a slotted spoon, transfer the peaches to the ice bath. Allow to cool completely, then gently peel the skins off, starting from the X cut.

TO MAKE A LATTICE TOP: Place a number of dough strips parallel to one another across the top of the pie. Fold every other strip up to about 1 inch from the pie dish rim and lay a strip perpendicular to the strips over the pie. Replace the folded-up strips down, and fold the alternate strips up. Lay another strip perpendicular over the pie. Repeat this pattern until you have a lattice pattern over the entire pie. Trim the overhang to a scant 1 inch and use your fingers to crimp the edges.

DOUBLE-CRUST PIE DOUGH

MAKES ENOUGH FOR
A DOUBLE-CRUST
9-INCH PIE

2 cups all-purpose flour

1 tablespoon cane sugar

1 teaspoon sea salt

10 tablespoons vegan stick
   butter, cut into small cubes

½ cup plus 1 to 2 tablespoons
   ice-cold water, as needed

1. In a bowl, whisk together the flour, sugar, and salt. Add the vegan butter and cut it into the flour using a pastry cutter (see Note). The result should be pea-size pieces blended with the flour.

2. Add the ice-cold water 2 tablespoons at a time and use a wooden spoon to stir. After adding ½ cup of the water, the dough should stick together when tested with your hands. If it seems too dry, add up to 2 more tablespoons ice-cold water.

3. Divide the dough into 2 equal portions, form into balls, and wrap them individually with parchment paper or plastic wrap. Refrigerate for at least 1 hour before rolling out.

4. Remove the chilled pie dough from the fridge. Let it sit on the counter for 10 minutes to soften before rolling out according to the recipe's directions.

NOTE: Alternatively, if you don't have a pastry cutter, you can pulse together the dry ingredients and vegan butter in a food processor, being careful not to overmix and heat the butter.

Cardamom Brown Sugar
POUND CAKE

My nana's star dessert is her signature pound cake. When I was a little girl a fancy birthday cake wouldn't please me; I had to have Nana's dense and buttery pound cake. I still adore Nana's pound cakes, which we have veganized, but I think of this cardamom brown sugar pound cake as the grown-up millennial version. Cardamom's pungent flavor is so unique—somewhat sweet and peppery, with notes of citrus. For the freshest taste, use a spice grinder to grind the cardamom seeds into a powder before using. You can also buy ground cardamom.

MAKES ONE 9 × 5-INCH LOAF

Vegan stick butter and flour, for the pan (optional)

1 cup plain unsweetened soy milk or other nondairy milk

1 tablespoon apple cider vinegar or distilled white vinegar

2 cups all-purpose flour

1½ teaspoons baking powder

½ teaspoon baking soda

½ teaspoon sea salt

1 teaspoon ground cardamom

1 teaspoon ground cinnamon

½ cup vegan cream cheese (Tofutti brand)

4 tablespoons vegan stick butter, at room temperature

1 cup packed light brown sugar

2 teaspoons pure vanilla extract

FOR SERVING

Vegan whipped cream (optional)

Fresh fruit (optional)

Fresh mint (optional)

1. Preheat the oven to 350°F. Grease and flour a 9 × 5-inch loaf pan or line it with parchment paper for easy removal.

2. In a small bowl, combine the soy milk and vinegar and set aside to curdle.

3. Sift the flour, baking powder, baking soda, salt, cardamom, and cinnamon into a bowl.

4. In a stand mixer fitted with the whisk (or in a bowl with a hand mixer), beat the cream cheese and butter until creamy. Add the brown sugar and continue to beat until fluffy.

5. Add the vanilla to the curdled soy milk mixture and pour into the mixer. Continue beating on low and slowly add the flour mixture. Once the batter is mixed (be careful not to overmix), pour it into the loaf pan and spread it evenly.

6. Bake until a toothpick inserted in the center of the loaf comes out clean, 50 to 55 minutes.

7. Let the loaf cool in the pan on a rack for 20 minutes, then remove the loaf from the pan and serve at room temperature. Serve with vegan whipped cream, fresh fruit, and mint, if desired.

Chocolate
PECAN PIE

I love celebrating springtime holidays like Easter and Mother's Day by serving slices of luxurious chocolate pecan pie. It took years to nail this recipe, and luckily I discovered that sweet potato puree is the perfect replacement for eggs in pecan pie. Not only does it give the pie body, it adds an earthy sweetness you didn't know pecan pie was missing. And everything is better with chocolate. I like using the vegan extra dark chocolate chips from Guittard, available at many gourmet grocery stores and online.

MAKES ONE 9-INCH PIE

Flaky Pie Dough (page 208)

1 cup mashed sweet potato (see Note)

3 tablespoons arrowroot powder or cornstarch

4 tablespoons vegan stick butter

¼ cup plain unsweetened soy milk or other nondairy milk

½ cup cane sugar

½ cup plus 2 tablespoons vegan dark chocolate chips or chopped baking chocolate

½ cup dark maple syrup

2 teaspoons pure vanilla extract

¼ teaspoon sea salt

2 cups chopped toasted pecans, plus more for garnish

Vegan whipped cream, for serving (optional)

NOTE: To get 1 cup smoothly mashed sweet potato, microwave or bake an 8-ounce sweet potato. Peel and mash with a fork.

1. Make and chill the pie dough as directed. About 10 minutes before you're ready to roll out the dough, let it sit on the counter to warm up.

2. Preheat the oven to 350°F. In a large bowl, combine the sweet potato puree and arrowroot powder. Set aside.

3. In a small saucepan, combine the butter, soy milk, sugar, chocolate chips, maple syrup, vanilla, and salt. Bring to a simmer, using a whisk to break up any clumps in the mixture, and cook until the chocolate chips have melted and all of the ingredients are blended into a sauce, about 3 minutes. Remove from the heat. Stir the pecans into the chocolate mixture.

4. Slowly pour the chocolate mixture into the bowl with the sweet potato and arrowroot and stir well. There should be no clumps.

5. Place the ball of pie dough on a flour-dusted smooth stone surface (if you don't have a stone surface use parchment paper). Use a floured rolling pin to roll the dough to ⅛ inch thick and 12 inches in diameter. Fit the dough into a 9-inch pie dish. Trim the overhang to a scant 1 inch and use your fingers to crimp the edges. Pour the filling into the prepared pie shell.

6. Bake until the top of the pie is dry, 45 to 50 minutes.

7. Remove from the oven and allow it to cool for at least 1 hour before serving. Top with vegan whipped cream and chopped toasted pecans, if desired.

FLAKY PIE DOUGH

This recipe, which relies on cold sticks of vegan butter to achieve maximum flakiness, is perfect for pies or quiches (see Leek Mushroom Quiche, page 50).

MAKES ENOUGH FOR ONE 9-INCH PIE

1¼ cups all-purpose flour

½ teaspoon sea salt

1½ teaspoons cane sugar

5 tablespoons vegan stick butter, cut into cubes

¼ cup plus 1 to 2 tablespoons ice-cold water, as needed

1. In a bowl, whisk together the flour, salt, and sugar.

2. Add the butter and use a pastry cutter (see Note, page 203) to incorporate into the flour until the mixture resembles coarse meal, with pea-size pieces of butter.

3. Add the ice-cold water 2 tablespoons at a time and use a wooden spoon to stir. After adding ¼ cup of the water, the dough should stick together when tested with your hands. If it seems too dry, add up to 2 more tablespoons of ice-cold water. Once the dough begins to hold together, form it into a tight ball.

4. Flatten the ball a bit (this will make it easier to roll out later) and wrap it in plastic wrap or parchment paper. Refrigerate for at least 1 hour.

5. Let the chilled dough sit on the counter for 10 minutes to soften before rolling out.

6. Roll out according to the recipe directions.

No-Bake Cherry Walnut CRUMBLE

Easy to make and not too shabby on the health benefits, the cherry walnut crumble is another family favorite. It's a terrific way to elevate cherries, which are tossed with balsamic vinegar and spread between layers of walnut and date crumble. I love enjoying this dessert in the summertime when cherries are in season (you can use thawed frozen cherries during the fall and winter). Pair it with Georgia Peach Ice Cream (page 196) for a cool, refreshing sweet treat.

SERVES 4

4 cups cherries, pitted

1 tablespoon balsamic vinegar

2½ cups walnuts, toasted or raw

1½ cups pitted Medjool dates (or other varieties of dates)

½ cup vegan dark chocolate chips

TO EASILY PIT CHERRIES: PLACE A STEMMED CHERRY OVER THE OPENING OF A SODA BOTTLE. USE A METAL STRAW TO PRESS STRAIGHT THROUGH THE TOP OF THE CHERRY. IT WILL PUSH THE PIT OUT OF THE BOTTOM OF THE CHERRY INTO THE BOTTLE.

1. In a bowl, toss the cherries with the balsamic vinegar. Set aside.

2. In a food processor, combine the walnuts, dates, and chocolate chips and pulse to chop just until the mixture has a very crumbly texture. Measure out one-third of it to use as a topping. Continue to blend the rest of the crumble for another 10 seconds. The mixture should hold together tightly in your hand. Be very careful not to overblend and make nut butter.

3. Pour the crumble into the bottom of an 8 × 8-inch or 9 × 9-inch baking dish. Press the mixture firmly into the bottom.

4. Layer the cherries into the baking dish. Cover with the chunky crumble that you set aside before.

5. Serve right away or refrigerate for the crust to firm.

Avocado Pineapple
ICE POPS

My daughter loves eating frozen desserts, but store-bought ones are far too sugary. I limit our consumption of sugary products, but that's okay because you can make delicious frozen desserts with fresh fruit. Avocados are rich in healthy fats and give these pops a terrific creamy texture. Use super-sweet pineapple for maximum flavor. Add a touch of lime to brighten these, and indulge in a frozen sweet treat that works as a snack or dessert.

MAKES 6 POPS

1 avocado, halved and pitted

2 cups chopped fresh pineapple (about ½ whole fruit)

1 tablespoon agave syrup (optional)

1½ tablespoons fresh lime juice

¼ cup shredded coconut, toasted (see Note)

IF YOU'VE GOT SOME OLD, DENTED AVOCADOS, THIS RECIPE IS A GREAT WAY TO USE THEM.

1. Scoop the avocado into a blender. Add the pineapple, agave (if using), and lime juice. Blend until creamy.

2. Pour into six 4-ounce ice pop molds. Top with toasted coconut.

3. Freeze overnight before serving.

NOTE: Spread the coconut on a small baking sheet and toast in a 350°F oven for about 5 minutes.

BETTER BEVERAGES

Down South, we love our iced teas and cold beverages. With temperatures breaking 100°F these days, Southerners are understandably gulping down everything that comes poured over ice, and I'm one of them. When I want to cool off, I enjoy a refreshing glass of Hibiscus Pineapple Skin Tea (page 219) or Peach Tea Soda (page 216).

And we love our cocktails! More than 90 percent of the time I sip on water (lots and lots of water) and herbal teas, but I certainly make room in the other 10 percent for an enticing cocktail or sugary mocktail. Like sugar, alcohol can have profound impacts on your health, so enjoy it in moderation for longevity and well-being.

But it would be remiss of me to not recognize how important socializing can be to our well-being, and so often dinner with family or chilling with friends includes an alcoholic beverage or two. The cocktails in this section are designed to impress your friends with unique and colorful twists on classics, like the Frozen Beet Margarita (page 224) and Dirt Candy Sour (page 228). I provide a number of options for alcohol-free beverages, and these days, online and at some liquor stores, you can find alcohol-free spirits of every kind. Cheers to vegan vibes!

Peach Tea
SODA

You can easily make your own fruity and delicious sodas at home with a few simple ingredients: fresh fruit, sugar, and sparkling water. I take this peach simple syrup to the next level by adding black tea, which provides bold flavor and the perfect amount of caffeine. I was inspired to make this peach tea soda by a spectacular blackberry tea soda I enjoyed at a wellness resort. It is the perfect combination of two beloved beverages: tea and soda. Homemade soda is also great because you can control how much flavored simple syrup you use, making it more or less sweet to suit your health goals. For the best results, make individual sodas on demand.

MAKES 8 SODAS

1 cup chopped peaches, plus more for garnish (optional)

½ cup cane sugar

1 tablespoon loose black tea leaves

Ice

Sparkling water or seltzer water

Mint, for garnish (optional)

1. In a small saucepan, combine the peaches and sugar and stir well. Let sit for 5 minutes.

2. Set the pan over medium heat and bring the peaches and sugar to a simmer. The sugar should melt completely within a couple of minutes.

3. Pour in ½ cup water and the black tea and stir well. Bring the syrup to a simmer, then reduce it to a low heat to very gently simmer for 20 minutes.

4. Strain the syrup and discard the solids. Allow the syrup at least 15 minutes to cool before making the sodas.

5. For each soda, fill an 8- to 12-ounce glass with ice. Add 1 to 2 tablespoons of the peach tea syrup. Pour in sparkling water and stir. Garnish with peaches and mint, if using, before serving.

Hibiscus
PINEAPPLE SKIN TEA

Pineapple peels deserve a second life! While not all fruit and veggie skins are edible, most peels are highly nutritious. I especially love pineapple peels. Like their yellow interior, pineapple peels come packed with loads of vitamin C, which helps to ward off illnesses and keep the body's immune system in check. Pineapple peels, as well as the ginger and turmeric in this tea, are also anti-inflammatory. Hibiscus, too, is rich in vitamin C, and is celebrated for its potential to reduce high blood pressure.

Pineapple skin tea is common in Jamaica and West Africa. This tea can be enjoyed hot or iced.

MAKES 8 CUPS

Skin and core of 1 whole organic pineapple (see Notes)

½ cup dried hibiscus flowers

1-inch knob fresh ginger, chopped

1½ teaspoons ground cloves or 5 whole cloves

1 cinnamon stick

½ teaspoon ground turmeric (optional)

½ cup coconut sugar, plus more to taste

1. In a large pot, combine the pineapple skin and core, 10 cups water, the hibiscus, ginger, cloves, cinnamon stick, and turmeric (if using). Bring to a boil. Reduce to a simmer, cover, and simmer over low heat for 45 minutes.

2. Remove from the heat and let the tea cool until safe enough to strain.

3. Strain into a pitcher or large jar, then stir in the sugar. Taste and add more sugar, if desired. Serve warm or over ice.

4. Keep the pineapple skin tea fresh by storing it in the refrigerator for up to 5 days. Cover the pitcher with plastic wrap to avoid absorbing fridge flavors.

NOTES:

- Make sure the pineapple is organic and also thoroughly wash the pineapple before peeling. Use a brush to get any debris out of the creases.
- Stir the tea each time before serving.
- If you want to serve the tea warm, reheat on the stove or in the microwave.

Green Girl GIMLET

My bestie, Patty, is funny, generous, and my-oh-my, does she know her agriculture. She owns a farm, Bedhead Plants, in Atlanta where she grows medicinal herbs. She made a version of this cocktail using herbs from her garden, and I've been hooked ever since. I'm a gin girl, but rum and vodka are equally yummy in this gimlet *(pictured opposite)*.

MAKES 2 COCKTAILS

4 ounces gin

1 ounce fresh lime juice

1 ounce Herbal Simple Syrup (page 239)

4 fresh basil leaves, torn

Ice

4 ounces lime sparkling water

Lime slices, for garnish (optional)

In a cocktail shaker, combine the gin, lime juice, herbal simple syrup, and basil leaves with ice. Shake vigorously for 20 seconds. Strain into two cocktail glasses filled with ice. Top with lime sparkling water and garnish with a slice of lime, if desired.

Lemongrass Cinnamon TEA

This anti-inflammatory tea feels like a spa visit in a cup. Lemongrass, which is known to assist with digestive issues and in lowering high blood pressure, is infused with cinnamon. Your home will smell like a soothing, peaceful oasis as the tea simmers on the stove. You can typically find fresh lemongrass stalks for a couple bucks at your local Asian grocery store. I enjoy drinking this tea iced, but you can serve it hot or cold, depending on your liking.

MAKES 6 CUPS

4 lemongrass stalks, outer leaves removed

3 cinnamon sticks

1. In a pot, bring 8 cups water to a boil.

2. Lay the lemongrass on the cutting board and cut the bottom piece off of each stalk. Using a rolling pin, smash the stalks to soften them and release some of the oils. Cut the stalks into 2-inch pieces, discarding the woody tops of the lemongrass.

3. Add the lemongrass pieces and cinnamon sticks to the boiling water. Reduce the heat to low, cover, and simmer for 30 minutes.

4. Remove from the heat and cool completely before straining the tea into a pitcher. Cover and refrigerate. Serve chilled.

Healthy
ORANGE FREEZE

Atlanta's classic local fast-food joint, the Varsity, is famous for their burgers. But as semi-vegetarians, my family's top choice was their Frosted Orange. Even my mom, who doesn't love sweets, loved this decadent blend of orange juice concentrate, Cool Whip, and condensed milk. To create a healthy vegan version, I use fresh unpasteurized orange juice (freshly squeezed is ideal), frozen banana, and nondairy milk. I add dates to sweeten and vanilla to give it the essence of that Varsity Frosted Orange that I remember so well.

MAKES 2 DRINKS

1 cup freshly squeezed orange juice (2 to 3 oranges), frozen in cubes (see Notes)

1 cup banana slices, frozen

1 cup plain unsweetened nondairy milk

3 Medjool dates, pitted (see Notes)

1 teaspoon pure vanilla extract or ½ teaspoon vanilla bean paste

Orange slices, for garnish (optional)

In a food processor, combine all the ingredients and blend until creamy. Transfer to glasses and serve garnished with an orange slice, if desired.

NOTES:

- To make frozen orange juice cubes, pour 1 cup freshly squeezed orange juice into an ice tray. When using a standard ice tray, 10 ice cubes is equivalent to 1 cup of juice.
- If the dates are very dry, soak them in a little water for 10 minutes before blending.

Frozen BEET MARGARITA

I thought I preferred my margaritas on the rocks until I tasted the delightful slushiness of this frozen beet margarita. Beets are certainly an unexpected ingredient for a margarita, but trust me on this one. Though it's just a little bit of beet, it makes this classic cocktail gorgeously pink, and it adds subtle earthiness: the perfect complement to tart and sweet. The accompanying beet sugar adds a pretty-in-pink sweet zestiness to the rim.

MAKES 2 COCKTAILS

Beet Sugar (recipe follows) or salt, for the rims

Lime wedge, for the rims

4 ounces tequila

4 ounces fresh lime juice

2 ounces triple sec

1 tablespoon agave syrup

1 small piece raw beet (about 1 inch long by ½ inch thick)

3 cups ice

Lime slices, for garnish

Mint, for garnish (optional)

1. Spread the beet sugar on a plate. Moisten the rims of two 9-ounce margarita glasses or 10-ounce old-fashioned glasses with the lime wedge and dip the rims in the beet sugar.

2. In a blender, combine the tequila, lime juice, triple sec, agave, beet, and ice. Blend until you have a smooth, icy consistency. Pour into the rimmed glasses and garnish with a slice of lime and mint (if using).

BEET SUGAR

This makes enough to rim two or three glasses. Scale it up if you're serving a crowd.

MAKES ABOUT 2 TABLESPOONS

2 tablespoons cane sugar or turbinado sugar

1 small piece raw beet (about 1 inch long by ½ inch thick)

Dash of grated lime zest

Place the sugar in a bowl. Use a Microplane or other very fine grating tool to grate about 1 teaspoon of the beet into the sugar. Add the lime zest and mix well.

Strawberry BRAMBLE

While I originally created this recipe for Valentine's Day, this drink is the perfect cocktail for spring and summer, too. Gin and muddled strawberries are a match made in heaven. With the addition of rose simple syrup, this perfectly pink cocktail is fragrant, fruity, and downright delicious.

As with any recipe that calls for fresh strawberries, you'll want to use the best of the best. Compromising on good strawberries really impacts the sweetness and flavor of a drink or dish, and we don't want that! Select the best strawberries you can from your grocery store, and if they're not in season, opt for frozen strawberries. Be sure to let them thaw before muddling to ensure you get their maximum flavor.

MAKES 2 COCKTAILS

4 fresh strawberries, hulled

1 cup cubed or crushed ice

4 ounces London dry gin

2 ounces fresh lemon juice (seedless)

1 ounce Rose Simple Syrup (page 239)

Crushed dry rose petals, for garnish (optional)

Strawberry or lemon slices, for garnish

1. Set 2 strawberries in the bottom of each of two cocktail glasses. Use a muddler to thoroughly mash the strawberries until you see a lot of strawberry juice at the bottom of the glasses and the pieces of fruit don't stick together in a clump. Top the strawberries with ice.

2. In an ice-filled cocktail shaker, combine the gin, lemon juice, and rose simple syrup. Close and shake vigorously. Pour into the glasses.

3. Sprinkle with some crushed dry rose petals, if desired. Garnish with a strawberry.

TO MAKE THIS ALCOHOL-FREE, USE WATER—STILL OR SPARKLING—IN PLACE OF GIN. IT'S ACTUALLY SUPER DELICIOUS AND REFRESHING, TOO.

Dirt Candy SOUR

This cocktail is, hands down, my favorite. There's just something about that unique mix of bourbon, sweet potato syrup, and Aperol, which adds a fantastic bitter orange taste that contrasts perfectly with the sweet potato. Of course, there are no egg whites atop this drink. In the vegan world, we use aquafaba, the liquid from cooked chickpeas. Aquafaba is nothing short of amazing in its ability to replace egg whites in myriad recipes. When whipped, aquafaba has a similar texture to egg whites. And don't worry—there's no chickpea flavor here. It adds the foamy texture of egg whites to the top of this resoundingly exceptional cocktail. Dirt Candy Sour is a fall-friendly cocktail, one that's great to serve at Thanksgiving, or to sip with friends huddled around the fireplace.

MAKES 2 COCKTAILS

1 ounce Sweet Potato Syrup (page 238)

1 ounce Aperol

2 ounces fresh lemon juice

2 ounces aquafaba (liquid from cooked or canned chickpeas)

4 ounces bourbon

Ice

Thin lemon slices, for garnish

Cherry, for garnish (optional)

1. In a cocktail shaker, combine the sweet potato syrup, Aperol, lemon juice, aquafaba, and bourbon and shake vigorously for 5 seconds.

2. Add ice and shake vigorously again for about 30 seconds. The harder you shake the foamier your cocktail will be.

3. Strain the cocktail into two 10-ounce old-fashioned glasses and garnish with a thin slice of lemon and a cherry (if using).

Pineapple Rose SANGRIA

I enjoyed my share of sangria during my days studying abroad in Madrid. Here I've taken the classic Spanish sipper and added my own twist, infusing the wine with a generous amount of strawberry and pineapple. Use a crisp Pinot Grigio or dry white or rosé wine that's not too sweet—we'll let the rose simple syrup take care of that!

SERVES 8

- ½ pineapple, chopped into small chunks
- 2 cups strawberries, chopped into small chunks
- ½ cup brandy (I use Martell)
- ½ cup Rose Simple Syrup (page 239)
- 2 (750 ml) bottles Pinot Grigio or other dry white or rosé wine (see Note)

In a tall pitcher, combine the pineapple and strawberries. Pour in the brandy and simple syrup and stir gently. Pour in both bottles of wine and stir well. Let the sangria chill in the fridge overnight for the best flavor, or for at least 1 hour. Fill the glasses with the sangria and a few scoops of the infused fruit to serve.

NOTE: IS ALL WINE VEGAN? Some wines are filtered, or "fined," using animal by-products like fish bladder (isinglass), gelatin, and egg whites. While these by-products are not thought to make their way into the final product, vegans may want to avoid wines produced this way. Many wines are labeled vegan, so you'll know no animal products were used in the "fining" process. You can also seek out wines that have not been filtered. Some wine lovers, even nonvegan, prefer these wines because they contain all of the wines' natural essence and flavor. Use Barnivore.com to find out if your favorite wine or beer is 100 percent vegan.

THE BEST SANGRIA HAS A CHANCE TO SIT OVERNIGHT SO THE FLAVORS CAN BLEND AND BALANCE. IF YOU DON'T HAVE TIME, AND NEED TO DRINK IT RIGHT AWAY (OR WITHIN AN HOUR), MUDDLE THE FRESH FRUIT WITH THE BRANDY AND SIMPLE SYRUP BEFORE ADDING THE WHITE WINE. ENJOY IT RIGHT AWAY, OR LET IT CHILL FOR AN HOUR BEFORE SERVING.

SAVE THESE SAUCES & FLAVOR-MAKERS

Let's face it: You're so much more likely to make a salad if the dressing is already made.

It's way easier and more motivating to chop up a bunch of corn, tomatoes, peaches, red onions, radishes, jalapeños, and herbs if you know they're going to be tossed into a perfectly sweet and salty Peach Miso Dressing (page 245), as you'll see in my Peach White Bean Salad (page 117).

All of these sauces can be made in advance, preserving the complex, aromatic flavors of the fresh ingredients at the heart of the sauce. Try the Mango Guacamole (page 245) for an evening gathering, and use sweet, nutty-feeling Tantalizing Tahini Chocolate Sauce (page 241) for my Wholesome Buckwheat Crepes (page 69). Charm even the most hesitant veggie eater with fruity vinaigrettes, and explore a range of sauces that can be paired with salads, sides, and even entrées.

Walnut **PARMESAN**

If I let her, Baby J would gladly eat a whole bowl of this cheesy vegan walnut parmesan. Luckily, I always keep a batch in the fridge for adding to pasta, pizza, salads, and beans. It's a simple blend of walnuts, nutritional yeast, and miso, with complex umami flavor. Though it only has a few ingredients, each one is packed with healthy goodness.

MAKES 1 CUP

1 cup walnuts, toasted or raw

¼ cup nutritional yeast

1 tablespoon mellow (white) miso

1 teaspoon extra-virgin olive oil

Sea salt to taste

In a food processor, combine all the ingredients and pulse until the texture of a chunky crumble. Store in an airtight container in the refrigerator for up to 2 weeks

Miso Tahini **SAUCE**

Not only can miso tahini sauce be used on the Dilly Broccoli Salad (page 121), but it's also a delicious spread for sandwiches, dip for raw veggies, and dressing for massaged kale salad.

MAKES ABOUT 1 CUP

⅓ cup tahini

¼ cup fresh lemon juice

1 tablespoon mellow (white) miso

1 tablespoon pure maple syrup or agave syrup

½ teaspoon smoked paprika

½ teaspoon ground cumin

¼ teaspoon cayenne pepper

In a small bowl, combine all the ingredients with 2 tablespoons water and use a whisk or fork to blend until smooth. Add more water to thin if necessary. Keep in mind it will thicken considerably once it is in the refrigerator. Store in an airtight container in the refrigerator for up to 5 days.

Perfect Every Time BROWN RICE

I've had a bit more luck using the Instant Pot than rice cookers when making rice, but you should choose the cooking vessel that feels most appropriate to you when making this easy and always perfect brown rice.

SERVES 6

2 cups brown rice

1 teaspoon any type of oil

½ teaspoon sea salt

Add the rice, 2½ cups water, the oil, and salt to the Instant Pot. Seal the Instant Pot and pressure cook for 24 minutes on high pressure. Let the pressure release naturally for 10 minutes, then quick-release the remaining pressure. Fluff and serve.

Sweet Potato PIE SPICE

Move over pumpkin pie spice! There's a new spice blend in town. I adore how cardamom gives this spice mix an elevated flare in a medley of earthy spices. Use this sweet potato pie spice anywhere you'd use pumpkin pie spice: in baking, morning oatmeal, coffee drinks, etc. It is an important ingredient in the Sweet Potato Syrup (page 238).

MAKES ABOUT ⅓ CUP

3 tablespoons ground cinnamon

2 teaspoons ground ginger

2 teaspoons freshly grated nutmeg

1½ teaspoons ground allspice

1 teaspoon ground cardamom

1 teaspoon ground cloves

In a small bowl, combine all the ingredients and stir well before storing in an airtight spice jar for up to 6 months.

Sweet Potato
SYRUP

What can't you do with rich and silky sweet potato syrup? Use this liquid gold to top Better Buttermilk Waffles (page 58), biscuits, pancakes, and crepes. Or make a sweet potato latte with it. Heck, you might even throw it into a cocktail—I use it in my Dirt Candy Sour (page 228) and it will blow your mind. It's super easy to make, and will stay fresh in the fridge for up to 1 month.

Don't discard the sweet potatoes after straining the syrup. Use the leftover pieces to make the Sweet Potato Butter (page 48).

MAKES 1 SCANT CUP

½ cup cane sugar

½ cup packed light brown sugar

1 (8-ounce) sweet potato, peeled and sliced

1 cinnamon stick

1 teaspoon Sweet Potato Pie Spice (page 237) or pumpkin pie spice

1 teaspoon grated fresh ginger

1 teaspoon pure vanilla extract

1. In a saucepan, combine all the ingredients with 1 cup water and bring to a simmer over medium-low heat. Simmer for 30 minutes, reducing heat if necessary. Remove from the heat, cover, and let sit for another 30 minutes.

2. Strain into a container, but save the sweet potato pieces to make Sweet Potato Butter (page 48). Store in the refrigerator for up to 1 month.

Rose SIMPLE SYRUP

Whether it's coffee, tea, or a refreshing cocktail, rose syrup adds a delightful pizzazz to the simplest of beverages and desserts. I use this rose simple syrup in the Strawberry Bramble (page 227) and Pineapple Rose Sangria (page 231). I also enjoy drizzling it into my morning latte and Hibiscus Pineapple Skin Tea (page 219).

Look for rose water at your local grocery store in the international foods aisle. You can also find it at international grocery stores, Middle Eastern and Indian grocery stores, or online.

MAKES 1 CUP

1 cup cane sugar
½ cup rose water

1. In a small saucepan, combine the sugar, rose water, and ½ cup water. Bring to a simmer over medium-low heat. Reduce the heat to low and continue to cook until the liquid has reduced by half and the syrup has reached a thicker consistency (similar to agave), about 20 minutes.

2. Remove from the heat, let cool, and store in a glass jar in the refrigerator for up to 1 month.

Herbal SIMPLE SYRUP

Simple syrups are the sweetest way to preserve the essence of fresh herbs. Syrups stay fresh in the refrigerator for up to a month, so you can enjoy the taste of summer long after the season is over. Use this herbal simple syrup in the Green Girl Gimlet (page 220), or pour into sparkling water for a refreshing soda. I love the combination of basil, mint, and rosemary, but this syrup lends itself to a number of fresh herbs: Think tarragon, marjoram, and even sage.

MAKES ½ CUP

1 cup cane sugar
10 fresh basil leaves, chopped
5 fresh mint leaves, chopped
1 sprig fresh rosemary

1. In a small saucepan, combine the sugar, 1 cup water, and the fresh herbs and bring to a simmer. Cook uncovered over medium-low heat until the simple syrup has reduced by about half, about 20 minutes.

2. Remove from the heat and strain the simple syrup through a fine-mesh sieve. Store in an airtight container in the refrigerator for up to 1 month.

Tantalizing
TAHINI CHOCOLATE SAUCE

My favorite culinary invention to come out of the Middle East is tahini: creamy dreamy sesame seed butter. Blend tahini with cocoa powder and dates to create this silky sauce. I usually make it to drizzle over Wholesome Buckwheat Crepes (page 69) and fresh fruit, but it is good enough to eat with a spoon. This sauce stores well in the refrigerator for up to 1 week, but beware: If you've got folks with a sweet tooth in the house, it'll go fast!

MAKES 1 CUP

- ½ cup tahini or other nut/seed butter
- 3 tablespoons soy or almond milk, plus more as needed
- 2 tablespoons pure maple syrup
- ½ cup pitted Medjool dates or soaked Deglet Noor dates
- ¼ cup unsweetened cocoa powder

In a food processor, combine all the ingredients and blend until smooth. Add more soy milk to thin if necessary. Store in an airtight container in the refrigerator for up to 1 week.

IF YOUR DATES ARE SUPER DRY, SOAK THEM IN THE SOY MILK TO SOFTEN FOR 20 MINUTES BEFORE BLENDING.

Peach SALSA

You can best believe that I am going to add fresh peaches to almost everything. Fruity peach salsa is amazing on Curried Red Bean Tacos (page 158) or served with crunchy tortilla chips. Use raw peaches and tomatoes for this salsa, or deepen the flavor by using roasted or grilled fruit.

MAKES 2 CUPS

1 large peach (unpeeled), minced (about ½ cup)

1 large tomato, minced (about ½ cup)

1 shallot or red onion, minced

¼ cup fresh cilantro, finely chopped

2 tablespoons fresh lime juice

¼ teaspoon cayenne pepper or ½ jalapeño pepper, minced, plus more to taste

½ teaspoon sea salt, plus more to taste

In a bowl, combine all the ingredients and toss well. (For a smoother salsa, pulse the ingredients in a blender or food processor until your desired consistency is reached.) Season to taste with more salt and/or cayenne pepper. Store in an airtight container in the refrigerator for up to 3 days.

Mango GUACAMOLE

I love the combination of salty and sweet, and this mango guacamole serves it up. I don't stray too far from a traditional guacamole here: a satisfying blend of avocado, diced onions, and cilantro seasoned with lime juice and salt. And then I like to add diced mango for a hint of sweetness. Enjoy this dip with your favorite chips or raw veggies for an afternoon snack, or use it to top the Curried Red Bean Tacos (page 158) or Teriyaki Tempeh Tacos (page 172).

MAKES 2 CUPS

2 avocados, cubed

½ cup diced mango

¼ cup diced red onion

½ cup chopped fresh cilantro

Juice of 2 limes

½ teaspoon sea salt

Fresno or other hot chile pepper, sliced, for garnish (optional)

In a medium bowl, combine the ingredients (except the garnish) and use a fork to mash until your desired texture is reached. (Alternatively, you can do this with a mortar and pestle.) Garnish with the pepper if using. Store in an airtight container in the refrigerator for up to 1 day.

Peach Miso DRESSING

This delightful dressing is amazing on beans, grains, and greens. It marries the sweetness of fresh peaches with the savory goodness of miso for a truly delicious dressing.

MAKES ABOUT 1 CUP

1 peach, diced

¼ cup extra-virgin olive oil

3 tablespoons apple cider vinegar

2 tablespoons mellow (white) miso

½ teaspoon sea salt, plus more to taste

½ teaspoon freshly ground black pepper, plus more to taste

In a blender, combine the peach, oil, vinegar, miso, salt, and pepper and blend until creamy. Season to taste with more salt and pepper. Store in the refrigerator in a glass jar for up to 3 days.

Niçoise DRESSING

Quick and simple—two of my favorite things—this dressing pairs with my Naked Niçoise Salad (page 114) but can be used to enliven many other savory salads and roasted vegetables. You've got two options here: Place all the ingredients together in a jar and shake, or whisk them in a bowl. Just make sure you achieve an emulsified, creamy texture.

MAKES ABOUT 1 CUP

¼ cup red wine vinegar

2½ tablespoons minced shallot or red onion

1 large garlic clove, minced and mashed

1 tablespoon Dijon mustard

1 tablespoon pure maple syrup

1 teaspoon dried thyme

½ teaspoon sea salt, or more to taste

⅓ cup extra-virgin olive oil

In a screw-top jar, combine all the ingredients and shake until emulsified. (Alternatively, in a bowl, whisk together all the ingredients except the oil. Slowly pour in the oil and continue whisking as you pour until emulsified and creamy.) Store in the jar in the refrigerator for up to 1 week.

Lemon VINAIGRETTE

This is an incredibly versatile vinaigrette. I almost always use it for my Fennel Beet Salad (page 112), but you can add this easy-to-make dressing to literally any salad.

MAKES ABOUT ¾ CUP

2 tablespoons fresh lemon juice

2 tablespoons apple cider vinegar

1 tablespoon Dijon mustard

2 teaspoons pure maple syrup or agave syrup

½ teaspoon freshly ground black pepper

½ teaspoon ground cumin or cumin seeds

1 garlic clove, minced

⅓ cup extra-virgin olive oil

In a screw-top jar, combine all the ingredients and shake vigorously until creamy. (Alternatively, in a bowl, whisk together all the ingredients except the oil. Slowly pour in the oil and continue whisking as you pour until emulsified and creamy.) Store in an airtight container in the refrigerator for up to 1 week.

Strawberry VINAIGRETTE

I can eat this strawberry vinaigrette with a spoon. For best results, use the most flavorful strawberries you can find when they are in season. If you can't get your hands on great fresh strawberries use frozen! Organic frozen strawberries are super sweet. Thaw them before adding to the vinaigrette.

MAKES ABOUT 1 CUP

½ cup hulled strawberries

2 tablespoons chopped shallot (about ¼ small shallot)

¼ cup red wine vinegar

1 tablespoon Dijon mustard

1 tablespoon pure maple syrup or agave syrup

½ teaspoon freshly ground black pepper

⅓ cup extra-virgin olive oil

In a blender, combine the strawberries, shallot, vinegar, mustard, maple syrup, and pepper and blend until creamy. With the blender on its lowest setting, slowly pour in the olive oil. Once creamy and emulsified, transfer to a jar and store in the refrigerator for up to 2 days.

Curry VINAIGRETTE

Curry vinaigrette explodes with bright, pungent flavor. Use on raw or roasted vegetables, or drizzle on top of an herby salad.

- ¼ cup apple cider vinegar
- 1½ tablespoons pure maple syrup
- 1 tablespoon Dijon mustard
- 2 teaspoons curry powder
- 1 teaspoon sea salt, plus more to taste
- 2 teaspoons freshly ground black pepper
- 1 teaspoon ground cumin
- ½ teaspoon Kashmiri chile or cayenne pepper (optional)
- ⅓ cup extra-virgin olive oil

In a screw-top jar, combine all the ingredients and shake vigorously. (Alternatively, in a bowl, whisk together all the ingredients except the oil. Slowly pour in the oil and continue whisking as you pour until emulsified and creamy.) Add more salt to taste. Store in the jar in the refrigerator for up to 1 week.

Pomegranate VINAIGRETTE

This vinaigrette has some *tang*, y'all! And that's exactly what I love about it. The acidic lime juice acts like a sort of cousin to the sour pomegranate. The inherent sweetness of pomegranate seeds cuts right through the acidity, resulting in a sweet, tangy dressing that is so darn good. This goes especially well with my Lovely Lentil Sweet Potato Salad (page 118), but you can get creative here and add this to any of your vegetable concoctions.

Find pomegranate molasses in the international foods aisle of your grocery store, at international or Middle Eastern grocery stores, and online.

MAKES ABOUT ¾ CUP

1 tablespoon pomegranate molasses

1 tablespoon pure maple syrup

2 tablespoons fresh lime juice or lemon juice

1 tablespoon apple cider vinegar

1 tablespoon Dijon mustard

½ teaspoon ground cumin

½ teaspoon freshly ground black pepper

¼ teaspoon ground cinnamon

¼ cup extra-virgin olive oil

In a screw-top jar, combine all the ingredients and shake thoroughly. (Alternatively, in a bowl, whisk together all the ingredients except the oil. Slowly pour in the oil and continue whisking as you pour until emulsified and creamy.) Store in the jar in the refrigerator for up to 1 week.

Acknowledgments

I wasn't sure if I could do it again. Like raising a child, it takes a village to write a book. And I thank God for my village. Throughout the process I leaned on my people to help me find clarity, creativity, confidence, and joy. From my editor to my recipe testers, I am grateful for you all.

To my daughter, Jorji: Thank you for your patience and love. Becoming your mother unlocked the best part of me. You inspire me to be my best self, and I hope I inspire you to do the same. This cookbook wouldn't have been possible without you. I could only dream of having a child as enthusiastic about eating and cooking as you are. You're a girl after my own heart, and my little partner in crime.

My MVP, Jess: I cannot thank you enough for your support during the process of writing this cookbook. You not only held down the Sweet Potato Soul blog and newsletter, you were also the best recipe tester and my most loyal cheerleader. Thank you for your grace, patience, and trust in me.

Tara, my amazing assistant: You have become a part of our family. Both Jorji and I thank you for making our lives easier. Thank you for your willingness to meet me where I'm at. Some days I needed you to entertain JJ while I worked, and other times you were deep in the process of recipe testing with me. You have helped foster a home in which creativity, passion, and joy can thrive.

My editor, Donna: It has been a pleasure and honor to work with you on our second cookbook together. You have inspired me to give my all to this process, and you've challenged me to stay committed to my why. I'm so blessed to have you on my team.

To my agent, Cindy: Thank you for believing in me and my vision. Even when I wasn't sure which direction to go, you were my advocate. When I didn't feel confident, you knew I had it in me.

To my nana: Thank you for all of the rich recipe ideas, and for worrying about this cookbook more than I did. I'll never forget my obligations when you are around to remind me. ;) I thank you for giving me a passion for cooking, eating, and feeding others. You've fed people for a lifetime, and now I'm blessed to be able to feed you.

To Chefs Pop and Tracy Grandma: Thank you for not only feeding Jorji and me delicious vegan food, but for inspiring so many of the recipes in this cookbook. How lucky am I to be a part of this family that loves food as much as I do? Thank you for introducing me to new ingredients, and always being willing to try my creations. You are two of my favorite chefs.

To my mom: It's rare to have a mother who daily reminds their child that they can do anything they put their mind to, while also being a shining example of what it means to work hard and follow your dreams. The example you gave me growing up is priceless, and absolutely crucial to the best parts of who I am today.

My prayer warrior, Aunt Anna: Thank you for praying for Jorji and me every day. We rest easy knowing that your love and prayer surround us, even hundreds of miles away.

To my beautiful friends and siblings: Thank you for always being open to trying my new recipes, even at the beginning of this journey when I had no idea what I was doing and the food was subpar. You've been so patient and understanding, as well as encouraging. Thank you for trusting me and always showing up.

This amazing city: Atlanta, thank you for welcoming me back after fifteen years beyond your borders. This city has shaped so much of who I am, and it continues to inspire me. When I moved back home, I felt like I was finally in the right place again. I felt like I could relax, and let creativity work its way through me. It's the sense of safety and belonging that has given me confidence and assurance that I could go through this journey of writing another cookbook.

To my recipe testers: None of you were paid to do this, but you showed up to test recipes that were still imperfect and unclear. I am so grateful for your trust and honesty. There's no way I'd be able to share these recipes with the world without your help. Thank you: Cathy Loup, Jessica Croel, Chris Homsey, Iesha Green, Karen Wallace-Douglas, Jessica Fox, Sharon Cirillo, Linda Pullen, Patty Dukes, Jule Fruehling, Becca Nelson, Shenique Seale, Justine Valentine, Jessica Kunkel, Rosie Miller, David Weiner, Jeff Stroud, Zach Burrus, and Abby Herman.

My incredible online audience and newsletter subscribers: Thank you for being dedicated supporters. You provided me with invaluable insight and feedback on everything from the direction of the cookbook to the title. Thank you for your patience and understanding as I wrote this cookbook. Even though I had to step away from regular posts to the blog, social media, and my YouTube channel, I knew your support would continue. As much as I love creating recipes and content that speaks to who I am, I do it to inspire and help you. Thank you.

To my photographer, Caitlin Bensel, and the whole creative team: Thank you for saying yes to this project. I am honored to see my recipes come to life in full color under your vision and direction.

To my yoga studio, Highland Yoga: You have no idea how much this practice of yoga has helped me to show up for myself, my family, and to write this cookbook. Turns out I'm at my best when I am regularly practicing yoga, and I couldn't do it without your fantastic teachers and community.

To the worldwide vegan community: Everyone of us plays a part in the growth of this lifestyle, which has now become mainstream. When I wrote my first cookbook, *Sweet Potato Soul*, veganism was still a niche movement. Now as *Vegan Vibes* is born, it enters a world that is hungrier than ever for plant-based recipes. I am especially thankful to those who continue to carry the torch for ethical veganism. There are still over ninety billion animals slaughtered for food annually. We have plenty of work left to do. The ripple effect of being vegan has proven powerful, so keep up the good work.

Index